BLACK AMERICANS AND THE SUPREME COURT SINCE EMANCIPATION

Betrayal or Protection?

Edited by ARNOLD M. PAUL
Michigan State University

read Brown

THIS WEEK read Plessy

NEXT week read sec 3&4

HOLT, RINEHART AND WINSTON
New York • Chicago • San Francisco • Atlanta
Dallas • Montreal • Toronto • London • Sydney

Cover photograph: United Press International

Library of Congress Catalog Card Number: 73–186567
ISBN: 0-03-084009-0
Printed in the United States of America
2 3 4 5 008 9 8 7 6 5 4 3 2 1

CONTENTS

Introduction 1

THE COLLAPSE OF RECONSTRUCTION GUARANTIES

EUGENE GRESSMAN—Postwar Revolution in Civil Rights—and Judicial Counter-Revolution 9
CHARLES WARREN—Judicial Conservatism Was Necessary 21
C. PETER MAGRATH—The Court and the Compromise of 1877 25
ROBERT J. HARRIS—The Court as Ally of the South 31

THE RETURN OF EQUAL PROTECTION FOR BLACKS

ALFRED H. KELLY—The Coming of *Brown* v. *Board of Education* 36
EDMOND CAHN—The School Cases: Based on Moral Values, Not Social Science 45
EUGENE COOK and WILLIAM I. POTTER—The Court Overstepped Its Role 51
JAMES F. BYRNES—The Court Must Be Curbed 56
HERBERT WECHSLER—The Court Ignored Neutral Principles 65
CHARLES L. BLACK, JR.—The Court Upheld the Constitution 69

AFTERMATH OF BROWN: EXPANSION, UPHEAVAL, AND THE STRUGGLE FOR ENFORCEMENT

ALBERT P. BLAUSTEIN and CLARENCE CLYDE FERGUSON, JR.—The Judicial Destruction of "Separate but Equal" 75
LOREN MILLER—"All Deliberate Speed" a Mistake 80
JACK GREENBERG—Civil Rights and Militant Protest: The Court as Teacher 85
ALEXANDER M. BICKEL—A Pessimistic View: *Brown* May Be Irrelevant 96
YALE KAMISAR—An Optimistic View: *Brown* and the Black Revolution 102

THE ROLE OF THE COURT IN PERSPECTIVE

LEWIS M. STEEL—Still a White Man's Court 106
ROBERT L. CARTER—Rhetoric and Reality: The Court's Middle Ground 113
ARTHUR KINOY—New Frontiers in the Struggle for Black Freedom 118

APPENDIX

Plessy v. *Ferguson* (and dissenting opinion) 123
Brown et al. v. *Board of Education of Topeka et al.* 131
Table of Cases 137
Guide to Further Reading 138

ESTIMATED POPULATION OF BLACK AMERICANS IN THE UNITED STATES IN 1950

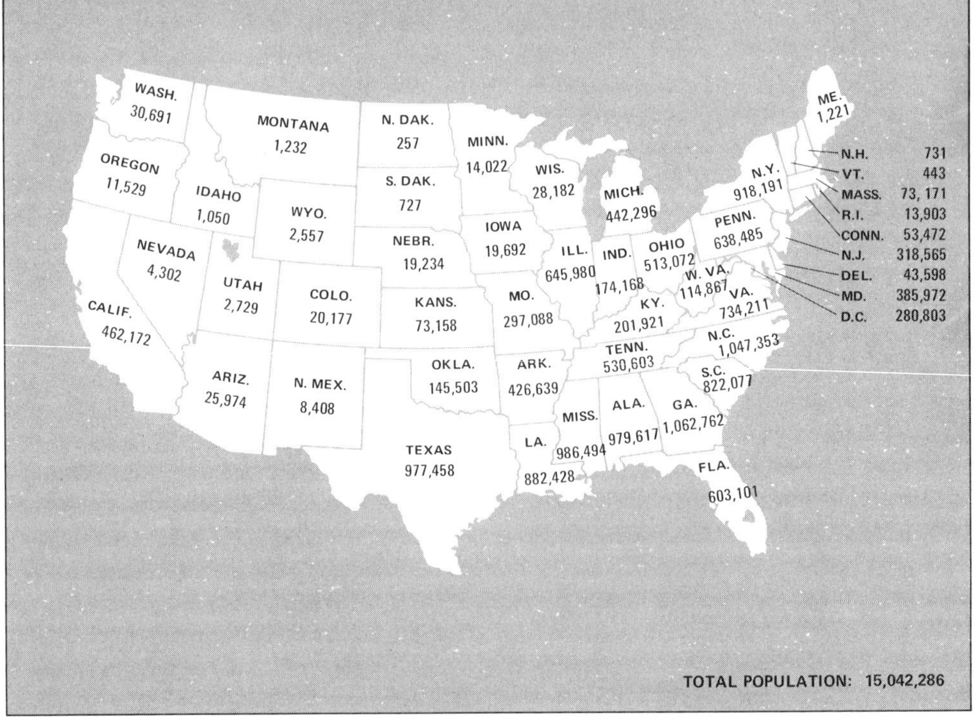

ESTIMATED POPULATION OF BLACK AMERICANS IN THE UNITED STATES IN 1970

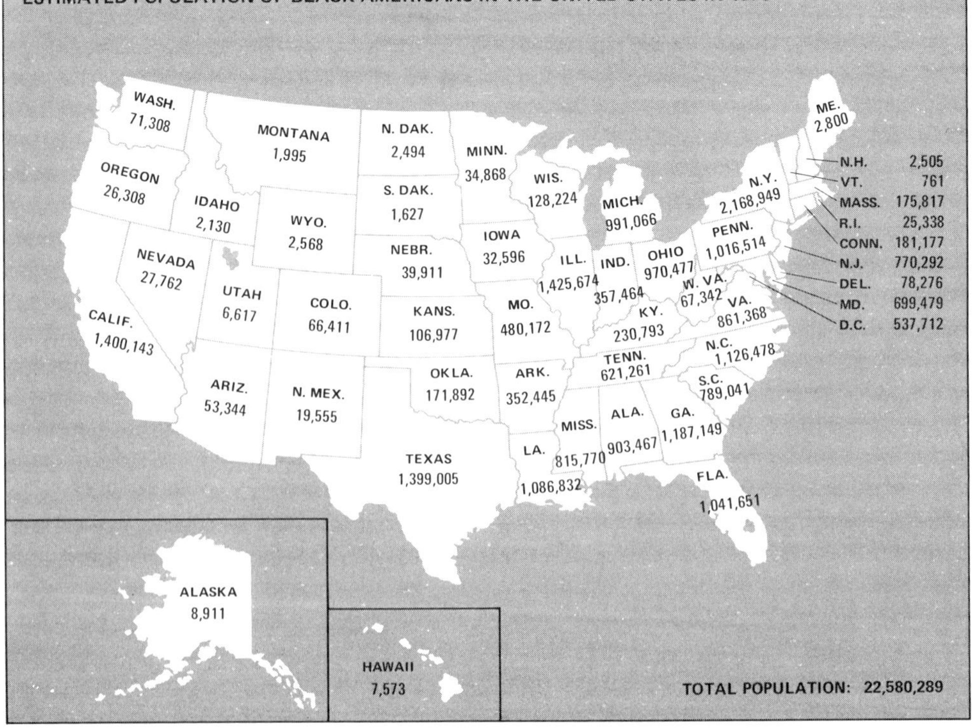

INTRODUCTION

In words that brooked of no uncertainty, the United States Supreme Court on October 29, 1969, ordered thirty-three Mississippi school districts "to terminate dual school systems at once and to operate now and hereafter only unitary schools." The standard of "all deliberate speed" for racial desegregation of schools (which the Court itself had propounded in 1955) was "no longer constitutionally permissible." The Court's opinion[1]—curt, blunt, unanimous—was the first important decision under the new Chief Justice, Warren Earl Burger, thus giving added authority to the Court's no-nonsense pronouncement. The decision clearly reached beyond the thirty-three recalcitrant Mississippi school districts to wherever racial discrimination in schools was still legally sanctioned, and indeed there was a veritable bursting of the dam in the rapidity of desegregation during the next year.[2]

The actual degree of effective *integration* was still uncertain, but the Supreme Court moved to meet this challenge too. On April 20, 1971, again unanimously, the Court sustained the use of extensive busing as a useful tool to "dismantle the dual school systems" of the South.[3] The Court's sweeping rulings also approved a variety of other "remedial adjustments" necessary to compensate for past inequalities—even if imposing "burdens on some."

The Supreme Court was not always like this. Back in 1857 in the famous *Dred Scott* case, the Court had ruled that no Negro, free or slave, could be a citizen of the United States or entitled to the protection of its laws. That the black man had "no rights which the white man was bound to respect" were the very words of Chief Justice Roger B. Taney.

When the Civil War ended, three constitutional amendments and five major enforcement laws were enacted, all designed to give black people not only freedom from chattel slavery but also the full, equal rights of American citizenship. The *Dred Scott* decision had been dramatically reversed by the national will.

On the bench of the Supreme Court, however, it seemed that little had

---

[1] *Alexander* v. *Holmes*. The decision was announced *per curiam* (an opinion for the whole Court rather than any one justice), emphasizing the summary disposition of the case.

[2] Black students attending integrated schools in the South jumped from about 20 percent to close to 40 percent.

[3] *Swann* v. *Charlotte—Mecklenburg Board of Education*.

changed. First, the Court gave a narrow interpretation to the meaning of United States citizenship (as distinguished from state citizenship); next, the Court emasculated or struck down congressional laws intended to protect blacks against mob violence and election frauds; then, in 1883 the Court annulled the Civil Rights Act of 1875, which made it a federal misdemeanor to discriminate, on account of race, in quasi-public facilities.

With congressional protective power destroyed, the Court turned around in the 1890s and bowed to state-imposed compulsory segregation. "Separate but equal" was the formula; grossly unequal became the practice. Similarly, the Court accepted the transparent discriminations against Negro voting in the so-called Mississippi Plan of 1890.

Thus, by 1900 the broad constitutional-legal structure for the protection of black citizenship and equality of rights was a mass of ruins, wrecked by the judicial ax. The black man soon sank into an oppressed caste status, not much removed from the era of slavery. The mass of the white public, North and South, accepted these developments with complacency, and Congress showed little interest after 1890.

For the next forty years, the Supreme Court remained mostly inhospitable to blacks' appeals, despite an occasional minor civil rights victory. Not until the 1940s did the Court show a sustained concern for the civil rights of Negroes. Then, in rapid succession, the Court struck down the white primary, made restrictive housing contracts legally unenforceable, and commenced the breakdown of segregation.

Brown v. *Board of Education* in 1954 was the watershed of the new judicial intervention in behalf of equal rights. For a unanimous Court, Chief Justice Earl Warren declared racially separate facilities for children in public schools "inherently unequal" and thereby shattered the legal rationale of segregation. Thereafter, a stream of federal cases consolidated and expanded the *Brown* principle, so that overt, governmentally sustained discrimination against black Americans became legally unsupportable wherever attacked in the courts.

In the meantime, the Court protected the rising tide of black militancy in the early 1960s when it struck down attempts to harass the NAACP (the chief legal arm of the civil rights movement) and reversed numerous convictions for peaceful sit-ins, protest parades, and so on. These demonstrations led, in turn, to the major federal civil rights laws of 1964 and 1965, which enacted national sanctions against racial discrimination in public accommodations (once again), and fashioned elaborate procedures to protect voting rights—a complete cycle from the passive, judicial-political acquiescence at the turn of the century.

Despite this new egalitarian trend, the Supreme Court has been accused of dilatory enforcement of key decisions, such as the long delays in school desegregation once tolerated under "all deliberate speed." Protection of protest actions also waned in the mid-sixties. Furthermore, in regard to the vast extent of private or de facto discrimination in schools, housing, employment, neighborhood services, police administration, and so on, the Court has moved cautiously or not at all.

The long historical sweep of the Supreme Court and the black American raises fundamental questions about the role of the Court. Has the Court mainly followed public opinion, largely negative to equality for blacks in the late nineteenth century, more positive in the mid-twentieth? Or has the Court led the way for public opinion, perhaps by consolidating an uncertain public consensus? Has the Court really been *significant?*

From another point of view, has the Court failed to live up to its imperative judicial responsibilities in behalf of constitutional rights and liberties? Taking the opposite view, can we fairly charge that, in its attempt to end discrimination, the Court has gone *beyond* its proper role, particularly in the highly controversial *Brown* opinion?

Looked at from the black man's perspective, in the long travail since Emancipation, has the Court been responsible for betrayal or protection?

The essays that follow take up these questions within broad chronological categories corresponding to the main time periods of "Court-black" history. The first group of selections considers the late nineteenth-century collapse of Reconstruction guaranties. The second group concentrates on the coming of the *Brown* decision and the controversies it spawned. The third group examines the developments after *Brown,* emphasizing civil rights expansion and the search for enforcement. The final group offers three interpretations of the long-term role of the Court.

Eugene Gressman leads off with a well-drawn presentation of the postwar constitutional amendments and the major congressional civil rights laws. He assesses their purposes and ideals, and then describes the main Court decisions that struck down the intentions of Congress. Gressman underscores the nationalist and libertarian motivations of the Reconstruction legislators, and he is sharply critical of the Supreme Court's "counter-revolution." Writing in 1952, when a new Court was serving the cause of civil rights in a more favorable climate of opinion, was Gressman perhaps too harsh on the old Court?

In the next selection Charles Warren discusses the Court's decisions from a traditional view. Warren agreed, from the perspective of the early 1920s, that the Court's opinions probably narrowed the intended scope of the postwar amendments, but he justifies the work of the Court as "wise" and "fortunate." The Court had removed the Negro question from politics and helped restore southern confidence in the federal government. Warren acknowledged that the Court decisions had left the former slaves without federal protection, but protection, he concludes, was properly the duty of the states. How does one explain an argument of this kind, even from a New England conservative, after two decades of numerous and notorious lynchings in the South?

A more modern defense of the Court is offered by C. Peter Magrath in the excerpt presented from his biography of Chief Justice Morrison R. Waite (1874–1888). Magrath attributes the Court's denial of the black man's claims to "the spirit of 1877," when a search for national harmony was the dominant mood. More clearly than Warren, Magrath deeply regrets the evil that soon befell the Negro (and he includes some moving quotations from federal agents), but he maintains that the justices of the Court, like many other prominent Americans, considered it their primary duty to promote sectional reconciliation—even at the price of the freedmen's rights. Is Magrath too tolerant of the Waite Court and its upholding of the "bargain" of 1877? Was it really necessary for the Court to go with the rest of the "Establishment"?

In the final selection for this period, Robert J. Harris roundly castigates the Court for its decisions on race relations, especially *Plessy* v. *Ferguson* (reprinted in the Appendix), which sanctioned compulsory segregation. The Court had emerged, Harris concludes, as an ally of the South. In contrast, he applauds Justice Harlan's famous dissent in *Plessy* (also in the Appendix) as historically, constitutionally, and morally correct. The contemporary reader will probably agree with Harris (and Justice Harlan), but whether the Court could have stemmed the tide of segregation in the 1890s, had it so chosen, is doubtful. Still, the question persists, was it right for the Court to reinforce that tide? Or did the justices simply share, as Harris implies, the intense racial stereotypes of their time?

Some sixty years later, the Supreme Court finally turned away from the *Plessy* doctrine of "separate but equal" and decisively rejected racial segregation. The great landmark case of *Brown* v. *Board of Education* (printed in the Appendix), which was applicable initially only to public schools, is the central subject of the second group of essays. Alfred H. Kelly, a constitutional historian who participated in NAACP strategy conferences on the case, describes the political and legal background leading up to *Brown*. Kelly emphasizes the new political potential of Negroes in the 1930s and the coming of a more sympathetic Supreme Court. He also gives much credit to the new litigation techniques developed by the NAACP, which he sees as the "cutting edge" of the many forces tending to break down segregation.

The *Brown* decision evoked bitter and continuing controversy, primarily from opponents of racial integration, but also, in a more restrained manner, from some legal scholars who believed the Court had abused its judicial discretion in order to obtain a desired result. The five selections following Kelly's background article present differing views of the *Brown* case.

In the first of these selections, Edmond Cahn, a legal scholar and philosopher, challenges the widespread assumption that Chief Justice Warren's opinion was based on the testimony of social scientists. Cahn criticizes the social scientists' so-called evidence as not scientific at all and warns that the fundamental rights of Negroes must rest on firmer ground. The Court achieved this objective, Cahn asserts, by solidly rooting its opinion in the nation's moral and constitutional philosophy. Has Cahn downgraded too much the significance of the social science evidence?

The second selection in this group is a joint article by Eugene Cook, attorney general of Georgia at the time of *Brown,* and William I. Potter, a Kansas City lawyer; they collaborate in a blistering attack on the Court's opinion, written obviously from a conservative southern viewpoint. Unlike Cahn, they insist that the Court did rely on social science testimony, and make many charges against the Court's use of it. Cook and Potter also denounce the Court for overturning precedents and disregarding states' rights. Clearly, to them "the old Constitution" had been betrayed for the mirage of Negro equality.

An even sharper challenge to the Court comes from former Supreme Court Justice James F. Byrnes, who was Governor of South Carolina at the time of *Brown.* His caustic critique of *Brown,* which climaxes with a call to "curb the Court," became the rallying standard for the growing attack on the Court from the Right. When the Court handed down a series of civil liberties cases in 1957 that reversed convictions of admitted Communists, attacks on the Court mounted to a dangerous crescendo, and Congress came close to passing legislation that would have severely restricted the Court's authority in certain types of cases.

The attempt to "curb" the Court failed in the late 1950s, partly because the right-wing southern conservative attack on the Court went too far. Criticism of the *Brown* decision, however, now appeared in unexpected circles. In a widely noted lecture at Harvard, Herbert Wechsler, a constitutional law professor from Columbia Law School, portrayed the Supreme Court as ignoring "neutral principles" in many of its decisions, including *Brown.* But is the Constitution neutral?

In the last selection of this group, the *Brown* decision is defended by Charles L. Black, a Texas-born professor at Yale Law School, who emphasizes the realities of segregated life in the South. The Court merely recognized what all the world knew, says Black (in his sparkling style), when it ruled that compulsory segregation *was* inequality, and, therefore, in violation of the Fourteenth Amendment.

The legal impetus from *Brown* spread rapidly to overthrow all forms of state-compelled segregation. Albert P. Blaustein and Clarence Clyde Ferguson show the sweeping impact of the case on southern municipal recreation facilities and then, most symbolically, on bus transportation. For it was in transportation that the separate but equal formula had received initial Supreme Court sanction; that doctrine was now smashed. And yet, as Blaustein and Ferguson show, the Court never did overrule *Plessy* in name—nor did the Court adopt Justice Harlan's great dissent.

While the principles of *Brown* were being extended from education to other public functions, the slow enforcement of *Brown* itself became a grave national issue. In the deep South particularly, outright state refusal to obey the Court's order and violence against civil rights advocates were the most dramatic and obvious acts of resistance. But more significant were the varied forms of delay and subterfuge fashioned by local school boards, state officials, and even some southern federal judges.

The selection by Loren Miller, who was a vice-president of the NAACP, tells the story of these delays, which Miller blames on the "all deliberate speed" formula of *Brown*. This had been announced by the Supreme Court in May 1955 in its second *Brown* opinion (*Brown II*), which explained the principles to govern enforcement. Under this standard, states Miller, the Supreme Court looked the other way for almost ten years while southern segregationists were encouraged to manufacture one device after another to forestall integration. Miller gives the Court the benefit of good intentions, but is he right in terming "all deliberate speed" a great mistake? Would other options have worked much better? Compare Miller's position with Greenberg's discussion of the same issue in the next selection.

Jack Greenberg's article is a fascinating study of the Court as teacher. Greenberg ties together the slow pace in the Court's enforcement of *Brown* with its repeated reversals of convictions of civil rights demonstrators. For the first ten years, the Court was forced to rely on the broad principles of its teaching that racial discrimination was unjust and immoral, while it waited for the country (and the politicians) to catch up. In the meantime, protest actions of young blacks, commencing with the 1960 sit-ins, spread rapidly in numbers and dimension. The protests became a powerful and dramatic reinforcement of the Court's teachings, and when demostrators were arrested, the Court protected and encouraged them by reversing convictions—although generally on minor technicalities.

Then in the mid-1960s the Court switched both ways. Reinforced by the Civil Rights Act of 1964, it began to press harder for implementation of *Brown*. At the same time, the Court became concerned with the rising level of "dissonance" (as Greenberg calls it) in the country, which encompassed such divisive issues as Vietnam and university reform, as well as racial equality. As a result, the Court permitted most convictions of demonstrators to stand, thus teaching a "law and order" lesson.

Greenberg's analysis is complex but is worth attentive study, and it raises important questions. Can we accept that the Court's decisions are motivated as much by the aim of teaching the public as by "finding" the law (as some lawyers put it)? Was the Court remiss in failing to insist on immediate enforcement of desegregation, no matter what the apparent difficulties or consequences? Why should civil rights protestors have more protection in one period than another, simply because the Court (or the "swing" justices of the Court) reacts negatively to rising national tension? For that matter, why should protestors over Vietnam or university reform have less protection than civil rights protestors?

The selections on the aftermath of *Brown*—expansion and enforcement—conclude with two directly opposing interpretations by prominent law professors.

Alexander Bickel, of Yale Law School, although supporting the original intent of *Brown* v. *Board of Education,* believes that the changing nature of the public school system, together with the disillusionment with integration expressed by some blacks, are making the *Brown* decision "irrelevant." But Yale Kamisar, of the University of Michigan Law School, points to the rapid increase in southern desegregation since 1965, and even more emphatically, to the great significance of *Brown* in opening the floodgates of the Black Revolution. Thus, Bickel sees the *Brown* decision as a probable failure in the long run, while Kamisar sees it as a tremendous success. Is it likely that both Bickel and Kamisar have overstated their arguments?

The final section presents long-term perspectives on the black man's experience with the Supreme Court since Emancipation. Lewis M. Steel, a lawyer with the NAACP, wrote a highly controversial article for the *New York Times* in October 1968, charging that the Supreme Court was then and always had been a white man's Court—the interest and convenience of whites invariably took precedence over the rights of blacks. He entitled his article "Nine Men in Black Who Think White." Steel was promptly dismissed from the NAACP legal staff, which thereupon resigned en masse. But the charges raised by Steel, which he spells out for every period of Court history since the Civil War, remain disturbing. Perhaps Steel was deliberately provocative in order to shake up liberal complacency about the Court. Is there, nevertheless, a core of truth to his accusations?

A more favorable view of the Court, though modified with criticism, appears in the next selection by Robert L. Carter, former general counsel of the NAACP (until his resignation over Steel's dismissal) Carter's article, which emphasizes the modern period of the Supreme Court, suggests that the Court has not always lived up to the principles it has proclaimed, say in *Brown* v. *Board of Education.* He agrees with some of the charges made by Steel, particularly the Court's refusal to approach the immense problem of de facto segregation. But he recognizes the Court's problems and welcomes its positive accomplishments. Like Kamisar, he sees its principal achievement, perhaps unintended, as the awakening of the average black to a realization that equality is his, not as a favor but as a right.

The last selection, by Arthur Kinoy of Rutgers Law School, serves well as a closing essay—and perhaps as a prophetic one. Kinoy's discussion revolves around the highly significant housing case of *Jones* v. *Mayer,* decided in June 1968, in which the Supreme Court resurrected the long-dormant Civil Rights Act of 1866. That act, the Court held, was constitutional under the Thirteenth Amendment, which abolished slavery and gave Congress the power to pass all laws necessary and proper to eradicate the "badges and incidents" of the slave system. Kinoy underscores the wording of the Court's opinion, which not only gave new life to the Thirteenth Amendment, as well as the Civil Rights Act of 1866, but also characterized the black ghetto as a "relic of slavery."

In the past, Kinoy suggests, the Court, like most Americans, could not bear to accept the full truth of the national betrayal of the promises of Emancipation. But in *Jones* v. *Mayer,* Kinoy concludes, the Court offers new hope, a new direction for the fulfillment of the promises of freedom. For in *Jones,* the Court proclaimed the breadth of the national power to end the heritage of slavery root and branch—and at the same time the Court recognized the bitter reality of American racism, which had perpetuated that heritage. How does Kinoy's article relate to the first article in our series (by Gressman)? Has the wheel of Court history gone full circle?

The Supreme Court as an institution has many responsibilities: to the continuity of the governmental system of which it is a key part; to the maintenance of its own supreme judicial power, which might not survive *certain* deeply unpopular positions; to the traditions of law and precedent.

Above all, however, the Supreme Court is a constitutional court. Its responsibilities are first to the Constitution, to the upholding of the fundamental principles of the Constitution. When the Court allows the pressures of the times to move it from its plain duty, and it accepts—in the words of Justice Harlan—the "thin disguise" of separate but equal, the Court has betrayed both the black man *and* the Constitution. When the Court reverses sixty years of precedents to restore the constitutional command of "equal protection of the laws," although this may offend the sensibilities of lawyers, the Court has adhered to its loftiest mission. It has protected both the black man *and* the Constitution.

Yet the justices are but men—and as Justice Henry Billings Brown, the author of the *Plessy* opinion, himself admitted (writing in 1912 after his retirement), the student of the Court's reports "perhaps to his surprise, will discover the same division of sentiment among the judges as among the people whom they are presumed to instruct."

Betrayal *and* protection—a mixed bag. But where the balance lies, each reader may determine for himself.

In the reprinted selections, footnotes appearing in the original sources have in general been omitted unless they contribute to the argument or better understanding of the selection.

Author of a widely used work on Supreme Court procedure, EUGENE GRESSMAN (b. 1917) served as law clerk from 1943 to 1948 to a noted civil libertarian on the Supreme Court, Justice Frank Murphy. Later he was a judge of the Appeal Tax Court, Montgomery County, Maryland, 1959–1962, and subsequently he entered private practice in Washington, D.C. Gressman's article in the June 1952 *Michigan Law Review* was the first in many years to give adequate attention to the failure of the old civil rights laws. His favorable picture of the postwar radical legislation and his powerful indictment of the Court's conservatism were years ahead of their time.*

Eugene Gressman

Postwar Revolution in Civil Rights—and Judicial Counter-Revolution

The enforcement by federal legislation of the constitutional rights of individuals is a story written largely in terms of confusion, distortion and frustration. Seldom, if ever, have the power and the purposes of legislation been rendered so impotent. Indeed, this story constitutes one of the saddest chapters in the historic struggle to effectuate the American ideal of freedom and equality for all.

Act I—The Legislative Prelude

Congressional implementation of the constitutional promises of freedom encompasses but a brief span of nine years, 1866 to 1875. Prior to that period the Constitution protected fundamental personal rights only against infringement by the federal government. This protection, embodied primarily in the first ten amendments, was not designed to be a sword or a shield against infringement either by the states or by individuals. And it was a protection essentially negative in character, permitting individuals to assert their rights only as a defense to some sort of governmental action. Such limited guarantees reflected the early fears of a powerful central government and the early reliance on the states as the protectors of the individual's rights and liberties.

The Civil War and its aftermath, however, wrought great changes in the constitutional framework of civil rights. The

*Eugene Gressman, "The Unhappy History of Civil Rights Legislation," *Michigan Law Review,* 50 (June 1952), 1323–1342. Reprinted by permission of the editors of the *Michigan Law Review.* Most footnotes omitted.

victory of the northern armies meant the effective end of slavery as a legalized institution. The slavery debate, which had so long embroiled the halls of Congress, receded into nothingness. In its place came a vigorous controversy over the federalist or nationalist tendencies of the abolitionists as they moved to consolidate their victory. This great controversy resulted in three new constitutional amendments and five congressional statutes supplementary thereto, all of which went beyond the immediate problems created by the emancipation of the Negro and caused a most profound shift in the status of the federal government relative to the civil rights of all inhabitants. The abolitionists and the Republican party reacted violently to the feeling of anti-federalism which had so long marked this area of human freedom. The states' rights doctrine suffer a complete albeit temporary eclipse. The national government no longer was viewed as the prime threat to civil liberties. Rather it was looked upon as the defender of the individual from assaults on his freedom stemming from state or private action. The nationalistic implications of the abolitionist movement came to their full fruition.

The first episode in this constitutional upheaval was the adoption and ratification of the Thirteenth Amendment, ratification occurring on December 18, 1865. This amendment abolished both slavery and involuntary servitude throughout the nation and gave Congress the power to make its provisions effective by appropriate legislation. Here for the first time was a constitutional command respecting individual freedom which was not confined in its reach to the federal government. It was also directed to the states. And, most significantly, it was directed to private individuals. As the Supreme Court noted, this amendment was "not a mere prohibition of State laws establishing or upholding slavery, but an absolute declaration that slavery or involuntary servitude shall not exist in any part of the United States."

The opponents of the Thirteenth Amendment attacked it as an unjustifiable invasion of the rights of the states and an undue extension of the power of the federal government. Indeed, it was argued that the amendment was so drastic in this respect as to destroy the federal character of the government and to be inconsistent with the whole spirit of the Constitution. These opponents assumed, as did the proponents, that the amendment was of a sweeping nature, that it went beyond the outlawry of personal bondage and guaranteed the emancipated Negro certain minimum rights, and that Congress would be enabled to safeguard and protect those rights by legislation. The guaranteed rights were thought to include equality before the law, protection in life and person, and free opportunity to live, work and move about. And the slavery to be abolished by the amendment was to include the incidents of the system which impaired and destroyed the civil rights of white persons. White citizens residing in the South and sympathizing with the Negro or the North were to be freed of the kidnapping, imprisoning, mobbing and murdering which the slavery system had spawned.

Thus, in the eyes of its supporters and opponents, the Thirteenth Amendment was the final step in the long campaign to end slavery and all its incidents. Not only were the Negro and his white friends to be protected in their privileges and civil liberties but the federal government was to be the effective means for achieving and perpetuating those ends through appropriate legislation.

But the need for legislative appendages

to the Thirteenth Amendment became almost immediately apparent. Something more than the idealistic words of the amendment was essential. Widespread atrocities against the free Negroes and their white friends continued in the South. Most southern legislatures enacted Black Codes, the many restrictions of which resulted in forcing Negroes to work for their former masters or other white men. The Negro in effect remained a slave in all but the constitutional sense. By virtue of these codes, he was "socially an outcast, industrially a serf, legally a separate and oppressed class."

The Reconstruction politicians became aroused at this resurgence of the Dred Scott philosophy, a philosophy which declared that Negroes were not citizens of the United States and had no rights which the white man was bound to respect. The 39th Congress, convening in December 1865, witnessed a variety of proposals, all designed to strike down the offensive Black Codes. . . .

The heart of this legislative program was a civil rights bill and a proposed amendment to the Freedmen's Bureau Act. These two bills represented the efforts of the amendment's framers, acting almost simultaneously with its ratification, to implement the intentions of the amendment. These two proposals were essentially the same, seeking to effectuate the amendment by protecting the civil rights and immunities of all people directly through the federal government. Section 1 of the civil rights bill and section 7 of the Freedmen's Bureau bill had identical lists of the civil rights to be guaranteed by the national government:

1. The right to make and enforce contracts;
2. The right to buy, sell and own realty and personalty;
3. The right to sue, be parties and give evidence; and
4. The right to full and equal benefit of all laws and proceedings for the security of persons and property.

Neither bill was designed exclusively for the benefit of Negroes. The Freedmen's Bureau bill extended the services of the bureau in protecting these rights to "refugees and freedmen in all parts of the United States," while the civil rights bill covered "the inhabitants of any state or territory of the United States." Moreover, both state action and state inaction fell within the ambit of these bills. And so did private, individual action. The evidence before Congress at this time was replete with instances of private individuals committing outrages and atrocities on freedmen and their white sympathizers.

Together, these bills effectively nationalized the civil rights of all inhabitants of the United States, white or colored. They culminated the abolitionist concept of the federal government as the protector of the essential principles of liberty. . . .

In the words of Senator Trumbull, the principal draftsman of the Thirteenth Amendment and the civil rights bill, under that amendment "Congress is bound to see that freedom is in fact secured to every person throughout the land; he must be fully protected in all his rights of person and property; and any legislation or any public sentiment which deprived any human being in the land of those great rights of liberty will be in defiance of the Constitution; and if the states and local authorities, by legislation or otherwise, deny those rights, it is incumbent on us to see that they are secured."

The civil rights bill became the Act of April 9, 1866, being enacted over the veto of President Johnson. It wrote into law that persons born in the United States and not subject to any foreign power were citizens of the United States, thereby overruling the *Dred Scott* decision. It further provided that such citizens, without regard to color, were entitled in every state and territory to the same right to contract, sue, give evidence, and take, hold and convey property, and to the equal benefit of all laws for the security of person and property, as was enjoyed by white citizens; and any person who under color of law caused any such civil right to be denied would be guilty of a federal offense. . . .

Litigation under the Civil Rights Act of 1866 found most courts willing to accept its constitutionality, although there were a few decisions to the contrary. But the doubts raised by the congressional opponents had a telling effect and many of the advocates of nationalization of civil rights felt none too secure Constitution-wise. Moreover, some of these advocates concluded that the rights secured by the 1866 act should be placed beyond the possibility of repeal by any later Congress. They felt that the centralizing of civil rights authority in the federal government should be made a permanent part of our constitutional way of life rather than remain dependent upon the fluctuating discretion of succeeding Congresses.

These doubts as to the adequacy of the Thirteenth Amendment and the 1866 act became so acute that it was soon deemed advisable to recast the provisions in a more detailed mold of a new constitutional amendment. Such was the motivating factor that led to the birth of the Fourteenth Amendment. Its proponents, fresh from the legislative battles of the Thirteenth Amendment, the 1866 Civil Rights Act and the Freedmen's Bureau bill, desired to solidify their intentions. They wished, by virtue of a new constitutional provision, to make certain that civil rights would be truly nationalized, that the federal government would inject itself into this realm that had hitherto been exclusively reserved to the states, and that all individuals would be protected in the full and equal enjoyment of the rights of person and property. More specifically, the provisions and implications of the 1866 act were meant to be incorporated into the Fourteenth Amendment.

It was also evident from the start that the framers of the Fourteenth Amendment had in mind more than the outlawing of state action which abused civil rights. The amendment sprang from the efforts of the congressional Joint Committee on Reconstruction. This committee studied the various suggestions made as to wording the new provision and also held formal hearings on the conditions then existing in the South. These hearings were significant in that they revealed that most of the abuses still being suffered by the Negro were at the hands of individual white persons rather than state governments or those acting under color of state law. Such private invasions of civil liberties were testified to by the vast majority of the 125 witnesses appearing before the committee. These hearings further demonstrated that the Negro was not alone in his tribulations; white persons who had supported the Union cause or who were bold enough to advocate civil rights for the Negro were also the victims of terrorism in the South. These factors were thus clearly in the minds of the committee members when they drafted the all-important first section of the Fourteenth Amendment. The demonstrated fact that violations of civil rights were primarily the product of individual rather than state action made it unreasonable for the committee to limit the scope of the amendment to state action. In fact, the committee's report, recommending "such changes of the organic law as shall determine the civil rights and privileges of all citizens in all parts of the republic," made plain the universal scope of the amendment. The subsequent debates in Congress implicitly assumed that individual action, not just state action, was covered by the amendment.

The various proposals for wording the Fourteenth Amendment ran from a simple prohibition of discrimination in state or national laws on account of race or color to a granting of power to Congress to secure to all persons "full protection in the enjoyment of life, liberty, and property." The contrast here was between a flat constitutional prohibition and a broad grant of power to Congress. But the basic idea of equal or full protection of the laws was present in all proposals. The final draft, as presented to the states for ratification, was something of a compromise. It contained both a constitutional prohibition and an allocation of power to Congress. The first section contained but eighty words, all of them designed to give national protection to persons or citizens in their natural rights:

> All persons born or naturalized in the United States, and subject to the jurisdiction thereof, are citizens of the United States and of the State wherein they reside. No State shall make or enforce any law which shall abridge the privileges or immunities of citizens of the United States; nor shall any State deprive any person of life, liberty, or property, without due process of law; nor deny to any person within its jurisdiction the equal protection of the laws.

This section was intended to be read in connection with the fifth section of the amendment, which gave Congress the power to enforce the amendment "by appropriate legislation."

The remarks in Congress concerning the first section, while meager, revealed the consistently broad intentions of the amendment's supporters. The early drafts had been in a more positive form in which Congress was directly authorized to secure to all persons the equal protection of the laws and to all citizens their privileges and immunities. Repeated statements on the floor of Congress revealed that this form of the equal protection clause related to the obligation of government to protect men in their natural rights and that such protection, when supplied, must be equal to all. But the final draft was much more negative in form. The prohibitions were made primarily on the states, with power being granted Congress to make such prohibitions effective by appropriate legislation. Just what was the purpose of this shift?

Congressional speakers made plain that section 1 of the final draft was designed to make certain that the Civil Rights Act of 1866 was constitutionally valid, a proposition which naturally drew forth the old charge that an undue amount of power was being concentrated in the federal government. But more than this was essential to the promoters of nationalized civil rights. Some future Congress might repeal the 1866 act and leave these rights short of federal protection. To eliminate that possibility required that the provisions of the act in some way be inserted into the new amendment itself. To do that entailed more than a simple grant of power to Congress to secure civil rights, which was what the early drafts of the amendment had done. So an outright prohibition was framed. Since Congress was already prohibited by other sections of the Constitution from encroaching upon these rights, the new prohibition was addressed to the states, combined with a grant of enforcement power to Congress. Such a prohibition was believed to be effective as to individual action, for if the state did not act to curb or punish the individual violators there would be state inaction of the type comprehended by the amendment, and Congress could then provide adequate remedies.

The first sentence of the amendment, making all persons born or naturalized in the United States "citizens of the United States and of the State wherein they reside," was added in the final stages of the amendment's development and was drawn from the 1866 act. It was feared that without such a definition of citizenship there might be an effort some day to take away from the Negro the protection of the amendment by declaring him not be a citizen, as the *Dred Scott* decision had done. And so the definition was added. National citizenship was thereby made primary and independent, while state citizenship was relegated to a secondary, derivative status. . . . The promoters of the Fourteenth Amendment were not interested in prohibiting the states from interfering with the narrow, technical relationships of a citizen to the federal government. They were desirous of precluding the states from impinging upon the rights to life, liberty and the pursuit of happiness. And they thought of those rights as necessarily belonging to national citizenship, rights which they labelled privileges and immunities.

In light of subsequent developments, it is unfortunate that the framers of the amendment did not give a more definite indication as to the privileges and immunities which were intended to be placed under the protective umbrella of the federal government. The phrase "privileges or immunities" referred plainly enough, in the framers' minds, to the fundamental rights of man, enumerated at least in part in the provisions of the 1866 act. They felt that the Declaration of Independence and the Constitution itself had made self-evident the great rights which attached to those in allegiance to the federal government. . . .

In any event, it was the privileges and immunities clause which the framers regarded as the core of section 1 of the amendment. The equal protection and due process clauses were treated by them as of secondary importance, as appendages to the protection afforded the privileges and immunities or the fundamental rights of national citizenship. Those clauses simply meant that in guaranteeing the basic human rights covered by the privileges and immunities clause, the federal government was to see to it that these rights were recognized and effectuated by the states on an equal basis and that any necessary deprivation of those rights by the states was in accordance with basic principles of procedural due process.

Such was the intended nature of the Fourteenth Amendment upon its ratification on July 28, 1868. Less than two years later, on March 30, 1870, the Fifteenth Amendment was ratified. This constitutional addition stated that "the right of citizens of the United States to vote shall not be denied or abridged by the United States or by any State on account of race, color, or previous condition of servitude," with power being given Congress to enforce the amendment by appropriate legislation.

Congress then made several bold efforts to enforce the Fourteenth and Fifteenth Amendments "by appropriate legislation." On May 31, 1870, a new Civil Rights Act was passed. This statute reenacted the 1866 act under the belief that whatever doubts may have previously existed as to constitutional validity were now removed by the Fourteenth Amendment. It also added criminal penalties for depriving anyone of the rights enumerated in the earlier law. In addition, the 1870 act made elaborate provisions to effectuate the right of free suffrage without distinction as to race, color or previous condition of servitude. Criminal sanctions were attached to any interference with an inhabitant's right to qualify as a voter, to register or to vote. A conspiracy section was added, punishing as a felony conspiracies to violate the statute or to injure, oppress, threaten or intimidate any citizen with intent to prevent or hinder his free exercise and enjoyment of any right or privilege granted or secured to him by the Constitution or laws of the United States.

On April 20, 1871, Congress passed another statute "to enforce the provisions of the Fourteenth Amendment to the Constitution." Known as the Ku Klux Klan Act, this statute was the indignant reaction of Congress to conditions in the southern states wherein the Klan and other lawless elements were rendering life and property insecure. Both civil and criminal penalties were established for the deprivation of rights under color of law. The pith of the act was section 2, making it an offense to "conspire together, or go in disguise upon the public highway or upon the premises of another for the purpose . . . of depriving any person or any class of persons of the equal protection of the laws, or equal privileges or immunities under the laws." If state authorities were unable or unwilling to prevent the deprivation of a constitutional right, and violence resulted, the President was empowered to take appropriate measures to suppress the violence. Moreover, the person whose civil rights were injured was given a civil cause of action against the officer who should have but did not protect him, a provision which was specifically directed against lynching and other forms of mob violence.

The capstone of the congressional civil rights program came on March 1, 1875, with the adoption of "An act to protect all citizens in their civil and legal rights." . . . Section 1 of the new law required all inns, public conveyances, theaters, and other places of public amusement to open their accommodations and privileges to "all persons within the jurisdiction of the United States," subject only to legal conditions applicable alike to citizens of every race and color, regardless of any previous condition of servitude. Section 2 made a violation of this provision a misdemeanor and gave the injured person the right to recover a $500 penalty for each offense. Federal courts were given exclusive jurisdiction over cases arising under this statute, with all cases being reviewable by the Supreme Court regardless of the sum of money involved.

Here was the most penetrating of all the civil rights statutes. It was confirmatory of the principles which motivated the adoption of the Thirteenth and Fourteenth Amendments. The Thirteenth Amendment, it will be recalled, was designed to do more than illegalize personal bondage. The intention was also to remove the badges and incidents of slavery and involuntary servitude. Freedom from slavery meant freedom to exercise civil rights without discrimination based upon race or previous condition of servitude. The 1875 statute was molded so as to effectuate that principle where discrimination was practiced by individuals in the exercise of public or quasi-public functions. Public conveyances, inns, theaters and other places of public amusement fell into the public or quasi-public category by their very nature and by virtue of the various governmental controls traditionally exercised over them. To be deprived of their services because of race or previous condition of servitude was truly thought to be a badge of slavery which could be eradicated. The 1875 law was also framed in accordance with the idealistic formula of the Fourteenth Amendment. Negroes were undeniably citizens of the United States and of the states wherein they resided by virtue of the first sentence of that amendment. Hence they were entitled to all the fundamental rights which national citizenship was thought to entail. . . .

Such were the congressional efforts from 1866 to 1875 to make secure the constitutional ideals of freedom and equality for all. Never before or since has there been so much important federal legislation regarding civil rights. The changes made by this series of enactments and constitutional additions were of a most significant nature, altering substantially the balance between state and federal power. Civil rights were conceived of as inherent ingredients of national citizenship and as such were entitled to federal protection. And that protection was to be accorded in an affirmative fashion. Congress made what "was probably the first attempt in the history of mankind to destroy the branches of slavery after its root had been destroyed." The federal government was given effective weapons to combat and defend against all who would deprive inhabitants of the United States of their rights to be free of inequalities and distinctions based on race, color and previous condition of servitude. These weapons were usable against both private individuals and those acting under color of state law.

As stated in Justice Swayne's dissent in the *Slaughterhouse Cases,* the Thirteenth, Fourteenth and Fifteenth Amendments, in the light of their true purposes, "are a new departure, and mark an important epoch in the constitutional history of the country. They trench directly upon the power of the States, and deeply affect those bodies. They are, in this respect, at the opposite pole from the first eleven. Fairly construed, these amendments may be said to rise to the dignity of a new Magna Charta."

Act II—The Judicial Coup d'Etat

But even before 1875, when Congress finished building this comprehensive structure of nationalized civil rights, corrosive elements were fast at work, elements which were eventually to leave the structure in ruins. The builders, fired with the combined zeal of the abolitionist movement, the post-war hatreds and the Reconstruction politics, had unfortunately left gaping structural weaknesses in their handiwork. They meant well. But their minds moved faster and more precisely than their hands. The result was that the loose, unprecise language that had been written into the constitutional additions, particularly the Fourteenth Amendment, permitted the enemies of nationalized civil rights to persuade the strict constructionists of the judiciary that the amendments did not say what the framers had meant them to say. Soon the bold motives and the brave arguments of the architects of the constitutional revolution in civil rights were forgotten under the din of a judicial rewriting of their efforts.

The most far-reaching incident of this counter-revolution came in 1873 in the *Slaughterhouse Cases.* By the narrow margin of five votes to four, the Supreme Court twisted beyond recognition the intended meaning of the crucial privileges and immunities clause of the Fourteenth Amendment. The effect was that the broad application of that amendment that was necessary to sustain the civil rights program of Congress was rendered impossible.

The *Slaughterhouse Cases* did not directly involve any of the civil rights statutes. But the constructon there given the privileges and immunities clause went to the very constitutional heart of those statutes. At immediate stake was a Louisiana law creating a monopoly in a single corporation for slaughtering animals. The Court upheld the validity of the monopoly grant on the ground that it was an appropriate exercise of the state's police power to protect the health of the community. In so doing, the Court was met with the argument that the Fourteenth Amendment had given primary national citizenship to Louisiana citizens and had provided that no state could abridge their privileges and immunities, among which was the privilege of engaging in the lawful business of slaughtering animals. The majority of the Court refused to accept this argument.

Justice Miller, speaking for the majority, said that only national citizenship received any protection from the privileges and immunities clause and that such national citizenship did not comprehend any of the fundamental rights of the individual. Those rights adhered only to state citizenship. To bring civil rights under the concept of national citizenship, as the framers intended, would in the Court's opinion be "so great a departure from the structure and spirit of our institution" and would so "fetter and degrade the State governments" that it would not be permitted "in the absence of language which expresses such purpose too clearly to admit of doubt."

National citizenship, as construed by the Court, included only those few rights which were beyond the possible reach of state citizenship and which grew out of "the relationship between the citizen and the national government, created by the Constitution and federal laws." Included were such as the right to travel to the national capitol, the right to sue in federal courts, the right to free access to the subtreasuries and the right to protection abroad and on the high seas. But these were rights that had no practical relationship to the cruel violence which marked the infringements of civil rights in the South and which gave rise to the amendment. They were rights that were already constitutionally protected from state infringement by virtue of the supremacy clause (art. IV, clause 2). In short, as Justice Field stated in his dissent, the privileges and immunities clause was rendered "a vain and idle enactment, which accomplished nothing, and most unnecessarily excited Congress and the people on its passage."

The decision in the *Slaughterhouse Cases* has never been reversed. The Fourteenth Amendment to this day has never recovered its life blood which the Court there extracted from it. Completely shattered was the privileges and immunities clause upon which rested the intricate pattern of nationally protected civil rights. The criminal sections of the civil rights statutes that relied on that clause to put teeth into such national protection were doomed. For all practical purposes the privileges and immunities clause passed into the realm of historical oddities. . . .

The judicially directed perversion of what the abolitionists tried to write into the Constitution did not stop with the *Slaughterhouse Cases.* Hard on the heels of that decision came *United States* v. *Cruikshank.* The Court there applied the *Slaughterhouse* doctrine directly to an alleged violation of a Negro's fundamental right to assemble. It held that an indictment under the conspiracy section of the 1870 act was defective in failing to allege that the right claimed to have been violated was one growing out of the Negro's relationship to the federal government. Unless an assemblage of Negroes were "for the purpose of petitioning Congress for a redress of grievances, or for anything else connected with the powers or the duties of the national government," a conspiracy to interfere with their right to assemble could not constitutionally come within the statutory scheme. In other words, the right to assemble peaceably is not a necessary attribute of national citizenship unless it is directly related in some way with the functions of the federal government. What the Court had done to the Fourteenth Amendment in the *Slaughterhouse Cases* it had now done to the civil rights legislation of Congress. In exercise of its power to enforce the amendment by appropriate legislation Congress was allowed to legislate only on the limited relationship between the citizen and the federal government.

But the *Cruikshank* case did even more damage to the civil rights program. The Court also announced that the first section of the Fourteenth Amendment consisted exclusively of restrictions upon the states and that it does not "add anything to the rights which one citizen has under the Constitution against another." The only obligation resting upon the United States, said the Court, was to see that the states did not deny their citizens the enjoyment of an equality of rights. "This the Amendment guarantees, but no more. The power of the national government is limited to the enforcement of this guaranty." Pursuing this thought still further in *Virginia* v. *Rives,* the Court restated the proposition: "The provisions of the Fourteenth Amendment of the Constitution . . . all have reference to State action exclusively, and not to any action of private individuals."

Knocked asunder thereby were all the high hopes of the amendment's framers that private action could be reached by federal legislation. It was private action, not state action, that had caused so much of the post-war bloodshed and atrocities in the South. It was private action, not state action, that had been the prime motivation for all the toil and debates that produced the Fourteenth Amendment and the surrounding legislation. Yet the framers had assumed too much and incorporated too little when they drafted the amendment. They failed to anticipate the judicial process of interpretation with its ever-present possibility of strict constructionism.

The elimination of private action from the reach of the Fourteenth Amendment meant the effective elimination of many of the provisions enacted by Congress pursuant to the fifth section. In *United States* v. *Harris,* for example, the Supreme Court declared void the important criminal conspiracy section of the Ku Klux Klan Act of 1871, which made it an offense to conspire to deprive any person of the equal protection of the laws or equal privileges or immunities under the laws. This was a provision aimed at lynchings and other mob actions of an individual or private nature. Since the Fourteenth Amendment was construed to concern only state action, it could not be used to sustain such a statutory proscription of private action. Nor could the Thirteenth Amendment be called upon to provide validity. That amendment, while applicable to private action, "simply abolished slavery and involuntary servitude."

The high point in the judicial negation of the abolitionists' labors came in 1883 in the celebrated *Civil Rights Cases.* At stake was the validity of the first two sections of the Civil Rights Act of 1875, which attempted to outlaw discrimination on grounds of race or color in the enjoyment of accommodations and privileges of public conveyances, inns, theaters and other places of public amusement. Those two sections were declared unconstitutional. Again it was pointed out that the Fourteenth Amendment affected only action by states and their agents and instrumentalities. A contrary interpretation "would be to make Congress take the place of State legislatures and to supersede them." Hence the Court majority could find no warrant for a statute such as this, since it was directed to individual owners of conveyances, inns, theaters, and the like who were found not to be agents of the states. Such proprietors were free to discriminate so long as their discriminatory actions had not been affirmatively authorized or permitted by state law.

The fifth section of the amendment, designed to be the deep well of needed legislative protection of basic civil rights, was held to give Congress nothing more than the power "to adopt appropriate legislation for correcting the effects" of the state laws and actions prohibited in the first section "and thus to render them effectually null, void and innocuous." The Court continued: "This is the legislative power conferred upon Congress, and this is the whole of it. It does not invest Congress with power to legislate upon subjects which are within the domain of state legislation."

The validity of the 1875 act under the Thirteenth Amendment fared no better. The Court conceded that the amendment was applicable to private individuals and it was willing to assume that Congress had power thereunder to outlaw all badges and incidents of slavery in the United States. But the Court was unable to say that the denial of admission to an inn or theater because of one's color or race subjected one to a form of servitude or fastened upon one any badge of slavery. Not even the 1866 act, enacted under the Thirteenth Amendment exclusively, attempted to cover the "social rights of man and races in the community" as the 1875 act was said to do.

Justice Harlan was alone in his brilliant but unavailing dissent.[1] He met the majority opinion at each and every point. But he could conclude only "that the substance and spirit of the recent amendments of the Constitution have been sacrificed by a subtle and ingenious verbal criticism. . . . Constitutional provisions, adopted in the interests of liberty, and for the purpose of securing, through national legislation, if need be, rights inhering in a state of freedom, and belonging to American citizenship, have been so construed as to defeat the ends the people desired to accomplish, which they attempted to accomplish, and which they supposed they had accomplished by changes in their fundamental law. . . . [T]he court has departed from the familiar rule requiring, in the interpretation of constitutional provisions, that full effect be given to the intent with which they were adopted." No more fitting description could be made of the Supreme Court's treatment of the civil rights amendments and legislation.

The pattern of narrow, debilitating construction was thus established. The scope and effectiveness of the civil rights statutes became progressively smaller as they were increasingly subjected to the cold water of the judicial process. Additional sections and provisions fell under the

[1] The report of the President's Committee on Civil Rights, TO SECURE THESE RIGHTS 105 (1947), stated of Justice Harlan's dissent: "So powerful a dissent remains a living force in constitutional law and is bound to be thoughtfully considered by any later Supreme Court when the validity of new civil rights laws comes before it for decision."

axe of unconstitutionality. All that the judiciary would recognize as valid were those provisions dealing with situations wherein state officials acted or misused their power or wherein rights were directly granted to private persons and guaranteed against individual infringement by the Constitution or federal laws.

The inevitable effect of these decisions was to transfer back to the states the prime responsibility for the protection of basic civil rights, a result which the legislators of 1866 to 1875 had expressly sought to prevent. The South was thereby enabled to create and perpetuate its rigid rules of segregation. Lynchings, race riots and other forms of unequal treatment were permitted to abound in the South and elsewhere without power in the federal government to intercede. The nation in fact entered upon an era of constitutional law, which Justice Harlan had feared, "when the rights of freedom and American citizenship cannot receive from the Nation that efficient protection which heretofore was unhesitatingly accorded to slavery and the rights of the master.". . .

A lawyer, historian, and lecturer, CHARLES WARREN (1868–1954) won the Pulitzer Prize in history in 1923 for his *The Supreme Court in United States History*, from which the selection below is taken. Though not a professional academic, he wrote a number of distinguished scholarly books and articles. Besides the work just mentioned, the most important are *Congress, the Constitution, and the Supreme Court* (1925) and *The Making of the Constitution* (1928). In all his books he took a strong federalist and nationalist position, supporting the powers of the Supreme Court against its liberal and radical critics. In this selection he defends the Court's civil rights decisions as necessary to regain the allegiance of the South. Does Warren indicate any view concerning the state of the Negro after the Court's decisions?*

Charles Warren

Judicial Conservatism Was Necessary

. . . The conservative and restricted interpretation which the Court, under Chief Justice Chase, had placed on the Privilege and Immunity Clause of the [Fourteenth] Amendment had given a warning to the extreme Reconstructionists that their hopes as to the validity of National Legislative protection to the negro might be dashed. When the additional Civil Rights Act of 1875, which directly penalized discrimination against the negro in public conveyances, hotels and elsewhere, was under debate in Congress, it was pointed out in the press that its validity was highly doubtful. "There can be little doubt," said the *Nation*, "that if it were not for the fatal habit we have fallen into since the war of regarding the Central Government practically above the law and the Constitution, whenever the negro is concerned, the mere suggestion of the constitutional points ought to have killed the bill forever. It is plainly unconstitutional. . . . In the interest of the negro, we trust that it may never reach the Court. Deeply as we sympathize with his wrongs, we have no expectation or hope of seeing them righted, by hounding on his old masters to acts of violence and lawlessness, by the passage of equally violent and lawless Acts of Congress. The Reconstruction period is ended, and the negro in future will occupy such a position as his industry and sobriety entitle him to. Such bills as the one we have been considering do nothing for him but turn his friends

*Charles Warren, *The Supreme Court in United States History* (2 vols. Boston: Little, Brown and Company, 1928), II, 600–618. Permission to reprint granted by the President and Fellows of Harvard College, Cambridge, Massachusetts. Footnotes omitted.

into enemies." The probable action of the Court was thus correctly prophesied; for within a year after this Civil Rights Act of 1875 passed, two decisions were rendered which entirely demolished the Radical Reconstructionist plan of protecting the rights of the negro by direct Federal legislation. On March 27, 1876, the Court, in *United States v. Reese* . . . held unconstitutional sections three and four of the earlier Civil Rights Enforcement Act of May 31, 1870, which penalized inspectors in State elections for refusing to receive and count votes and for obstructing any citizen from voting. In an opinion rendered by Chief Justice Waite, the Court held that under the Fifteenth Amendment, Congress had only power to enforce "by appropriate legislation" the right to exemption from discrimination in the exercise of the elective franchise on account of race, color or previous condition of servitude; that the statute in question was not confined to such a limited class of discrimination, but extended broadly to all discriminations and obstructions; that, so construed, it was an unconstitutional interference with the rights of the States. . . . Concomitant with this case, the Court rendered another decision which came as a heavy blow to those who were seeking to protect the negro voter. In *United States* v. *Cruikshank* . . . indictments had been found for conspiracy under section six of the statute; . . . Frauds and violence against the negroes in Louisiana State elections were involved in this case; and the defendants were charged with conspiring to prevent citizens in the enjoyment of their right to peaceably assemble with others, of their right to petition for redress of grievances, of their right to bear arms and of their right to vote; also with conspiring to falsely imprison and murder and thus deprive citizens of their lives and liberty without due process of law. . . . The Court held that the various rights so set up were not rights which citizens enjoyed by virtue of, or which were secured to them by, the Constitution of the United States; and hence, the actions set forth in the indictment did not come within the purview of the statute. . . . The right to vote was held to come from the States only, and it was only right of exemption from discrimination on account of race or color under the Fifteenth Amendment, which came from the United States. Inasmuch as the indictments did not allege such discrimination, they could not be upheld. "We may suspect," said the Court, "that race was the cause of the hostility, but it is not so averred."

The practical effect of these decisions was to leave the Federal statutes almost wholly ineffective to protect the negro, in view of the construction of the Amendments adopted by the Court, the lack of adequate legislation in the Southern states, and the extremely limited number of rights which the Court deemed inherent in a citizen of the United States, *as such,* under the Constitution. The decisions, nevertheless, were believed by all, except the Radical opponents of the South, to be wise and to open the door for more sane and liberal methods of dealing with the negro problem. . . .

The Radical Reconstructionists and their press saw, with anger and dismay, their whole scheme of legislation overthrown; and, as one party organ said, under the Court's construction, the statute was "only a pretense, keeping a promise to the colored man's ear and breaking it to his hope," and "if the Amendments, intended to secure all citizens of the United States from legal discriminations on account of color, fail to express their intention, the blunder is unprecedented.". . .

Viewed in historical perspective now, however, there can be no question that the decisions in these cases were most fortunate. They largely eliminated from National politics the negro question which had so long embittered Congressional debates; they relegated the burden and the duty of protecting the negro to the States, to whom they properly belonged; and they served to restore confidence in the National Court in the Southern States. As an eminent Southern lawyer has said: "When the decision was reached and the prisoners were released, the utmost joy succeeded [in Louisiana], and with it a return of confidence which gave best hopes for the future." . . .

A year after these decisions, President Hayes partially adopted the policy of leaving the South to work out its problems free from National interference, by withdrawing the regular army from Louisiana and South Carolina in April, 1877. An attempt by the Democratic Congress to repeal the Civil Rights Enforcement Acts was vetoed in 1877 by the President; but the Democratic success in the election of 1878 brought about a two years' fight for such repeal, and a bill was actually passed, as a rider to an Appropriation Act, forbidding the United States marshals to use military forces in the execution of election laws. It was not until 1894, under President Cleveland, that the chief obnoxious provisions of the Enforcement Acts were finally abolished.

Meanwhile, the extent to which the Fourteenth Amendment could be invoked for the protection of the negro was being further explained by other decisions of the Court. In 1880, in *Strauder* v. *West Virginia* . . . the Court reiterated that the chief design of the Amendment "was to protect an emancipated race and to strike down all possible legal discriminations"; and it held that a State statute which confined jury duty to white persons violated the Amendment, by failing to secure to negroes the equal protection of the laws guaranteed to them by the National law and Constitution. . . .

In 1883, however, the Court . . . practically put an end to attempts on the part of the Federal Government to settle the negro question by means of indictments in the Federal Courts. In *United States* v. *Harris* . . . which involved the constitutionality of section two of the Ku Klux Act of April 20, 1871, making it criminal for two or more persons to conspire or go in disguise upon the highway or upon another's premises for the purpose of depriving any persons of the equal protection of the laws and privileges and immunities under the laws, the Court held the section invalid, as unwarranted by the provisions of any of the Amendments, which, in granting to Congress the power to enforce their provisions, did not authorize Congress to legislate directly as to the acts of private persons. In the *Civil Rights Cases*, . . . decided October 15, 1883, the Civil Rights Act of March 1, 1875, was finally held unconstitutional. This statute had made it a crime for any person to deny full and equal enjoyment of the accommodation of inns, public conveyances and places of public amusement. The Court, through Judge Bradley, held the law to be beyond the power of Congress. . . . The Court further held that refusal of accommodation to a negro could not be justly regarded as imposing any badge of slavery or servitude upon him; and it said that "it would be running the slavery argument into the ground, to make it apply to every act of discrimination which a person may see fit to make as to the guest he will entertain"; hence the statute could not be upheld as a proper means of enforcing the Thirteenth Amendment. An interesting and vivacious dissenting opinion was given by Judge Harlan, who regarded the statute as clearly valid under the Thirteenth Amendment, and said that he could not "resist the conclusion that the substance and spirit of the recent Amendments of the Constitution have been sacrificed by a subtle and ingenious verbal criticism."

. . . That the interpretation given by the Court to the Amendments was a surprise to many statesmen, and a disappointment to those who saw, or thought they saw, in them a more comprehensive chart of liberty, has been frequently pointed out. "It was information that was new to the framers . . . when they were told that by those Amendments it was not intended to add anything to the rights of one citizen as against another; that it was not designed to enable Congress to legislate affirmatively or directly for the protection of civil rights, . . . It was information that was new, as well as unwelcome, that the provisions creating National citizenship and prohibiting the abridgement of the privileges thereof . . . added nothing to existing rights, but simply provided additional guarantees for such as already existed." Nevertheless, as a historian of the Court has well said: "Now, after the lapse of years, when the temper and spirit in which the text of the Amendments was penned have cooled and the views of men have matured, it is seen that the value of the Court as the great conservative department of the Government was never greater than then."

C. PETER MAGRATH (b. 1933) is dean and professor of political science at the University of Nebraska. Magrath's detailed and sympathetic biography of Chief Justice Morrison R. Waite shows Waite as essentially a moderate traditional conservative. In the selection below, Magrath explains that Waite and his Court shared in the national desire for reconciliation, especially after the Hayes–Tilden disputed election and the Compromise of 1877. Waite himself was also a strong believer in states' rights under the traditional federal system. Does this mean that the Waite Court (Harlan excepted) was prepared deliberately to undo the work of the Reconstruction Congresses?*

C. Peter Magrath

The Court and the Compromise of 1877

[Chief Justice] Waite's fear of a possible hostile reaction [to the *Cruikshank* and *Reese* cases] was groundless. The Republican New York *Times,* which three years earlier had blasted the Grant Parish Riot as a "fiendish deed," endorsed the decisions and spoke of "the admirable clearness and emphasis of the opinions." Whitelaw Reid's New York *Tribune* told its readers that the Enforcement Act was the "odious" product of a "greedy and malignant partisanship." The influential Springfield *Republican* also nodded approvingly, and, though somewhat fearful that the decision might encourage abuses against the Negro, the Chicago *Tribune* felt no hesitation in praising the opinions for a "clearness of thought and trimness of expression" which "will commend the new Chief-Justice to the confidence of his countrymen." So favorable was Northern reaction that the Richmond *Enquirer* ran an editorial lauding "the improved temper of the North" as a "return to reason."

Congressional reaction also spoke volumes. A scant decade before, the Supreme Court had been an object of suspicion, censured and threatened by the then ascendant Radicals. . . . *Cruikshank* and *Reese* would have provoked outraged howls in the 1860's; in 1876 Congress accepted them with the mildest of taps on the Court's wrist.

*Reprinted with permission of The Macmillan Company from *Morrison R. Waite: The Triumph of Character,* by C. Peter Magrath. © by Peter C. Magrath, 1963. Pp. 130–134; 137–139; 141–145; and 149. Footnotes omitted.

While the *Cruikshank* case drastically narrowed the scope of permissible civil rights legislation, the decisions seemingly left intact congressional power to prevent voting discrimination. Early in the summer of 1876 Senate Republicans forced passage of a bill reenacting the provisions voided in *Reese,* explicitly confining their operation to denials based on race. But a resurgent Democracy firmly controlled the House and there was no chance of the bill becoming law; it was not even introduced in the lower chamber. . . . The really striking feature of the Senate's behavior was its gentlemanly deference to the Court, its willingness to accept the idea that it, rather than the judges, was to blame for the flaws in the Enforcement Act. One Republican, Indiana's Oliver P. Morton, described the decisions as regrettable and vague, but even his remarks lacked sting. 1876 was an era—not a decade—removed from 1866. In 1876 there was no acrimonious denunciation of the Bench, no Thad Stevens to rail against judicial infamy, though perhaps his ghost stirred uneasily.

Where Congress acquiesced and Republican editors described the decisions as wise, Democratic and Southern newspapers reacted with undisguised glee. . . . Some, as did the New Orleans *Time,* took time to explain what the decisions meant for the Negro: "The colored suffragan, if not already conscious of the fact, must soon know that his prerogatives, under the constitution as amended, are no greater than those of any other citizen."

Just what prerogatives Negroes enjoyed in the eyes of white Southerners became evident in the years after 1876. Negro voting dwindled steadily as the whites regained total political domination in the states of the Old South. Obviously the Supreme Court's decisions in *United States* v. *Cruikshank* and *United States* v. *Reese* were not the sole causes, being but one of the elements in a much larger picture which included the North's felt need for reconciliation—a need which found political expression in the famous Compromise of 1877. Within this context *Cruikshank* and *Reese* assume significance in arranging one of the essential conditions for North-South reconciliation: the ending of meaningful political participation by the Negro.

It had been difficult enough before 1876 to enforce the voting rights of Negroes, convictions occurring in only twenty per cent of the cases; following the decisions the task became impossible. *Reese* and *Cruikshank* themselves were test cases upon which depended the fate of numerous prosecutions. In 1875 over two hundred prosecutions were started in the South, in 1878 only twenty-five. Fear of reprisal kept many Negroes from the polls, and those who went usually failed to get their votes counted. State officials naturally encouraged violations, and *Reese* and *Cruikshank* hampered the efforts of the United States attorneys. They stand for "the classical theory of an imperium of imperio," one of them complained in 1879. . . . This same attorney, the federal attorney in Charleston, South Carolina, gave a vivid description of his plight:

> I have been forced by the unfortunate condition here, to give to Reese et al and Cruikshank et al my severest study. I made last spring a careful abstract with notes, of these and all kindred cases and came to the conclusion then, which is much stronger now, that with the single exception of a few sections, relating to the elections of federal officers, the federal election laws are a delusion and farce. . . . If red shirts [a term for white bands] break up meetings by violence, there is no remedy, unless it can be proved to have been done on account of race &c, which cant be

proved; . . . It is hard to sit quietly and see such things, with the powerful arm of the Government, bound in conscience to protect its citizens, tied behind its back by these decisions. With colored men crowding my office, it is hard to make them understand my utter helplessness. . . .

I have not registered yet, and although I always do, feel like it would be wasting that much time. Suppose I vote, will it be counted and if I cant protect myself, how can I protect my friend of African descent. . . .

Thus did the Supreme Court's decisions have their impact. In practical terms they show that the Court, in facing the Southern question, marched in step with the national mood. . . . The Court that emasculated the Enforcement Acts and the war amendments was a Republican Court; its principal architects in these cases—Judges Waite, Miller and Bradley—were Northerners and Republicans whose credentials were unimpeachable. To suggest that they consciously fashioned a policy of conciliation would be impossible to prove and unjust to their motives . . . to Waite, a judge consistently devoted to the idea of broad state powers in all areas, there was "no escape" from the Court's conclusions.

More often than not, however, the national environment gradually finds expression in the Supreme Court's decisions. Judges live and breathe in the atmosphere of their day, and in 1876 reconciliation was in the air. "The day of our complete deliverance," the Richmond *Enquirer* hopefully proclaimed, "may be still longer postponed, but it will come at last . . ." *United States* v. *Cruikshank* and *United States* v. *Reese* were the opening phases of the Compromise of 1877—heralding the day of "complete deliverance," which, for the white South, was just around the corner. . . .

Even while Northerners and Southerners visited Philadelphia [at the Centennial Celebration of 1876] to mingle as Americans and gaze at the fruits of the new industrial order . . . the nation faced and resolved its most serious crisis since 1861. The crisis was the Disputed Election of 1876; its resolution, the Compromise of 1877. Only the bare bones of these events need be noted. As their candidate to succeed Grant the two parties nominated men who shared much in common: Samuel J. Tilden and Rutherford B. Hayes were political moderates and men of integrity; both could wear the mantle of "reform," and both were equally acceptable to the men of Wall Street. National politics remained nonetheless largely sectional, and Republicans, including Hayes, who favored a mild Southern policy, still waved the bloody shirt furiously. For his part, Tilden had a good record as New York's Democratic governor, making the outcome doubtful and the campaign an absorbing one. . . .

On November 8 the American people learned that Samuel Tilden had carried enough Northern states and most of the South to gain a tiny majority of the popular vote. South Carolina, Louisiana, and Florida, however, were nominally controlled by the Republicans and here conflict arose. Without electoral votes from at least one of these states Tilden lacked a majority; with the votes from all three Hayes had the necessary majority—185 to 184. In all but form the white Democracy controlled these states and claimed to be legitimately in power; the upshot was competing state governments which filed conflicting election returns. Adding to the confusion, which included charges of Democratic intimidation of Negro voters and countercharges of lawful interferences by federal troops on behalf of the Republicans, was the fact of divided government in Washington. Because Republicans controlled the Senate and Democrats the House, a count of the electoral vote became impossible. Finally, in late January, 1877, a Democrat-sponsored bill to create a special Electoral Commission to pass on the disputed returns picked up enough Republican support to get through Congress. After wading through the legal morass spawned by the fight for the Presidency, the Commission, composed of ten congressmen and five Supreme Court justices—Clifford, Field, Miller, Strong, and Bradley—divided along straight party lines and recommended that Congress certify the Republican electors. . . .

Southern Democratic cooperation was essential to the peaceful installation of Hayes, and to obtain it North and South struck a bargain. Most superficially, the bargin involved the sort of horse trading common to American politics: in return for their cooperation in seating Hayes and their promise not to mistreat the Negro, Southerners were to be rewarded with the withdrawal of federal troops and the recognition of the Democratic governments in South Carolina and Louisiana. Actually, as C. Vann Woodward's research shows, the Compromise of 1877 was considerably more than a simple political deal. . . . Federally-sponsored railroad construction and remission of the Negro to the control of the states were among the inducements offered the South. In turn, Republicans would benefit by becoming a truly national party, acquiring a stability which would make it better able to defend capitalism against the disturbing influences of the various Western heresies propounded by agrarians, Greenbackers, and silverites. . . .

As these events and adjustments took place the Supreme Court was no idle spectator. At one level the justices gave Hayes the Presidency. Five of them served on the Electoral Commission and from their ranks came the odd vote, Judge Bradley's, which made an eight to seven majority for the Republican candidate. Were this all, the commission's vote would mark only an isolated incident in Court history . . but the Waite Court's involvement in the social and political adjustments of the late nineteenth century went much deeper. . . .

. . . With the Southern states firmly in white hands, the federal government remained the Negro's last hope for civil rights protection. To be sure, the realities of the Compromise of 1877 made prospects for positive federal action on his behalf as dim as the rapidly fading memory of Charles Sumner. Still, the Negro and such loyal supporters as Robert Ingersoll and Wendell Phillips might at least hope that the principle of federal intervention would survive, to be reasserted again in some future, more hospitable period.

Any such hopes came to an end in 1883. In *United States* v. *Harris* the justices voided section two of the Enforcement Act of 1871, a provision which aimed at Ku-Klux activities by making it a crime for two or more persons to conspire or go in disguise upon a highway or another person's premises for the purpose of depriving them of the equal protection of the law or their privileges and immunities. This, said the Court, exceeded the authority conferred by the war amendments; Congress lacked power to legislate directly as to the acts of private persons. . . . Simultaneously with *Harris* the Court upheld an Alabama law making adultery or fornication between Negro and white a more serious crime than the identical offenses committed by two members of the same race. This, it declared, did not violate the Fourteenth Amendment's equal protection clause because the law applied equally to both races.

It was, however, the *Civil Rights Cases* (1883) nullifying the Civil Rights Acts of 1875, which guaranteed equal accommodations in inns, public conveyances, and places of public amusement, that pleased the South most and best signifies the Supreme Court's role as constitutional guardian of the Compromise of 1877. While in both North and South the act was often violated, there was no firm pattern of anti-Negro discrimination during the seventies and eighties. They were scarcely accepted as social equals, yet it was not uncommon to see Southern Negroes, particularly in the cities, mingling with whites in streetcars, restaurants, saloons, and theaters. The Civil Rights Act encouraged such nondiscrimination and, perhaps most important, stood as a symbol: to the Negro for his aspirations, to the white Southerner for the rigors of Reconstruction.

In voiding the act Justice Bradley, speaking for seven of his brethren, made explicit what in *Cruikshank* had been implicit. The Fourteenth Amendment "does not authorize Congress to create a code of municipal law for the regulation of private rights; but to provide modes of redress against the operation of State laws, and the action of State officers, executive or judicial, when these are subversive of the fundamental rights specified in the amendment." The Thirteenth Amendment was also irrelevant. Applying its prohibition against involuntary servitude "to every act of discrimination which a person may see fit to make as to the guests he will entertain, or as to the people he will take into his coach or cab or car, or admit to his concert or theatre," he declared, "would be running the slavery argument into the ground." . . . And finally he expressed a concluding thought on the subject of civil rights legislation:

> When a man has emerged from slavery, and by the aid of beneficent legislation has shaken off the inseparable concomitants of that State, there must be some stage in the progress of his elevation when he takes the rank of a mere citizen, and ceases to be the special favorite of the laws, and when his rights as a citizen, or a man, are to be protected in the ordinary modes by which other men's rights are protected.

Clearly, the welcome mat was not out for Negroes on their way to the Supreme Court.

Only one judge dissented, ex-slaveholder John Marshall Harlan, appointed to the Court by President Hayes in 1877 as a representative of the South. His thirty-four page opinion, attacking the majority for its "narrow and artificial" reading of the amendments which destroyed their "substance and spirit" by "a subtle and ingenious verbal criticism," ranks among the powerful dissents of Court history. To accept the majority's narrow concept of "state action," Harlan argued, reduced the amendments to delusive, "splendid baubles." He rejected Bradley's implied distinction between "social" and "civil" rights, insisting that the act aimed solely to protect legal rights. A colored citizen's right, he wrote, "to use the accommodations of a public highway, upon the same terms as are permitted to white citizens, is no more a social right than his right, under the law, to use the public streets of a city or town." . . .

Harlan closed by calling Bradley's description of the Negro as a special favorite of the laws "scarcely just":

> The statute of 1875, now adjudged to be unconstitutional, is for the benefit of every race and color. What the nation, through Congress, has sought to accomplish in reference to that race, is—what had already been done in every State of the Union for the white race—to secure and protect rights belonging to them as freemen and citizens.

However much the dissent may appeal today, in 1883 Justice Harlan was but a minority of one. Beyond the bench a few voices protested. Colonel Ingersoll denounced the decision for allowing "a contemptible white man to trample upon a good colored man," saying the country needed "another constitutional amendment or a new Court." At scattered places in the North Negro ministers presided over protest meetings. . . . Frederick Douglass, the early Negro leader and orator . . . attacked the decision as "a concession to prejudice" and contrary to Christianity, the Declaration of Independence, and the spirit of the age.

Douglass was vainly invoking an age that had passed with Thad Stevens and Charles Sumner. The North's most influential papers rushed to embrace the decision, . . .

As the century drew to a close, whites, North and South, considered the Negro question settled. Looking upon him as inferior in ability and unfit for self-government . . . Northerners came to believe that white supremacy was in the best interest of both races. Certainly it was in the best interest of Northern capital which flowed steadily into the South.

While a glance at the daily newspaper is sufficient reminder that the Negro question is anything but settled, the Compromise of 1877 proved enduring enough to restore Southern stability and so open the South to the capitalism that was the order of the day. However unfortunate, the nineteenth century Negro's low social and economic status made inevitable his dominance by the better trained and organized whites. Only the determined use of federal force could have given him an element of political security, and after 1877 any willingness to sustain such force totally disappeared in the North. Instead it wanted reunion; the Hayes-Tilden election crisis provided the excuse for the desired accommodation —an accommodation which had as one of its essential elements the remission of the Negro's destiny to the states. The Supreme Court saw to it that the bargain was not violated.

ROBERT J. HARRIS (b. 1907) is a professor of political science at the University of Virginia and a former Dean of the Faculty of Arts & Science. Born in Tennessee and educated at Vanderbilt, the University of Illinois, and Princeton, Harris has been sharply critical of racial segregation and discrimination. His book *The Quest for Equality* (1960) is a study of the origins and development of the Equal Protection Clause of the Fourteenth Amendment. Harris takes to task the Supreme Court for its distortions of the clear constitutional intentions of the authors of the Fourteenth Amendment. The South regained in constitutional law what it had lost on the battlefield; and, says Harris, it failed miserably to make constructive use of that unexpected victory.*

Robert J. Harris

The Court as Ally of the South

The last and one of the most important developments in judicial application of the equal protection clause in the nineteenth century was the emergence of the equal but separate formula in 1896 to sustain state laws compelling racial segregation in transportation, schools, and other public facilities, whether maintained by private owners or public authorities. Segregation by law played an insignificant role in the South prior to the Civil War, because custom and the concomitants of slavery were more than adequate in their own way to control race relations. Segregation laws, accordingly, were a northern import insofar as they were an outgrowth of the statutes of many northern states imposing serious disabilities on free Negroes as a class. . . .

. . . General segregation by law in the South did not become important until the 1890's, when one southern legislature after another began to enact a wide variety of statutes compelling separation of the races. This was not in response to any spontaneous public demand, but because of the clamor of demagogues who endeavored to outdo each other in running for office against the Negro as a fictitious opponent. Their purpose was both to get into office and to suppress Populist ideas among poor whites by throwing them a crumb of consolation in the idea that independently of their wretched poverty they were white and thereby better than the Negro, who in the future would be kept "in his place" by law.

✓ Low

* Robert J. Harris, *The Quest for Equality* (Baton Rouge: Louisiana State University Press, 1960), pp. 96–103; 107–108. Reprinted by permission of Louisiana State University Press. Footnotes omitted.

The equal but separate formula originally was neither a constitutional provision nor a judicial gloss on the Constitution. The formula first came to the attention of the Supreme Court in *Louisville, N. O. & T. Ry.* v. *Mississippi,* which involved a Mississippi statute requiring all passenger trains to provide "equal but separate facilities for the white and colored races." The Court sustained the measure on the ground that the act was not a regulation of interstate commerce and made no reference to equal protection.

It was not until six years later that the formula received judicial sanction in the face of the equal protection clause in *Plessy* v. *Ferguson,* in which the Court sustained a Louisiana statute requiring railroads to provide "equal but separate" accommodations for white and colored passengers. In an opinion redolent with sociological speculation, permeated with theories of social Darwinism, and carrying overtones of white racial supremacy as scientific truth, Justice Henry Billings Brown, as spokesman for the Court, found the statue valid as imposing no involuntary servitude under the Thirteenth Amendment and no illegal discrimination under the Fourteenth. He declared: "A statute which implies merely a legal distinction between the white and colored races—a distinction which is founded in the color of the two races, and which must always exist so long as white men are distinguished from the other race by color—has no tendency to destroy the legal equality of the two races, or re-establish a state of involuntary servitude."

From this assumption, inconsistent within itself and contrary to the facts of social life, Justice Brown argued that although the purpose of the Fourteenth Amendment was "undoubtedly to enforce the absolute equality of the two races before the law," it could not have been intended in the nature of things "to abolish distinctions based upon color, or to enforce social, as distinguished from political, equality. . . ." Here Justice Brown distorted constitutional history and departed from earlier precedents. If there was one clear intention of the framers of the Fourteenth Amendment, it was to abolish all legal distinctions based on color and in no sense to enforce political equality except in a most indirect way. The reference to social equality is wholly irrelevant, for social equality, as Justice Harlan forcefully indicated in his dissent, is not produced merely because two people ride side by side in the same train or sit together in a jury box.

Segregation laws, Justice Brown continued with sociological confidence, "do not necessarily imply the inferiority of either race to the other," and are a reasonable exercise of the state's police power. He cited the existence of separate schools as the most common type of segregation and invoked as his principal authority for the validity of segregation the case of *Roberts* v. *City of Boston,* in which Massachusetts' Chief Justice Lemuel Shaw rejected Charles Sumner's eloquent plea for equality before the law and sustained the power of the city of Boston to maintain separate schools for Negroes. The Roberts case, however, was hardly good authority. It antedated the Civil War and was repudiated by the Massachusetts legislature in 1855 in a statute prohibiting school segregation. After citing more relevant cases the Justice returned to his distinction between laws "interfering with the political equality of the negro" and those requiring segregation of the races in public places. Moreover, the Court found that the validity of all such legislation depends on its reasonableness and, making another departure from previous cases and history, contended that the legislature, in determining reasonableness, "is at liberty to act with reference to the established usages, customs, and traditions of the people, and with a view to the promotion of their comfort, and the preservation of the public peace and good order."

Justice Brown finally detected two fallacies in Plessy's argument. One was the assumption that segregation branded the Negro with a badge of inferiority, an assumption which could be true only because the colored race placed that interpretation on it. The other fallacy was the assumption that "social prejudices may be overcome by legislation, and that equal rights cannot be secured to the negro except by an enforced commingling of the two races." These arguments consist not only of dubious psychology in attributing inferiority exclusively to a state of mind, but also of poor logic in confusing the absence of segregation with the elimination of social prejudices and the enforced commingling of the races. Then, upon assumptions founded in social Darwinism, Justice Brown extolled the inefficacy of law as a means of social control of race relations by intoning: "Legislation is powerless to eradicate racial instincts or to abolish distinctions based upon physical differences, and the attempt to do so can only result in accentuating the difficulties of the present situation. If the civil and political rights of both races be equal, one cannot be inferior to the other civilly or politically. If one race be inferior to the other socially, the Constitution of the United States cannot put them upon the same plane." Here Justice Brown's jurisprudence is no better than his history, sociology, or psychology. It may be true, as the poet said, that "stone walls do not a prison make, nor iron bars a cage," but, supplemented by armed guards, they provide a very effective substitute. The fact is, of course, that laws do change customs and traditions even to the extent of uprooting them. Law and its penal sanctions have indeed changed the most stubborn of customs with respect to the legal status of Negroes.

The opinion of the Court in *Plessy* v. *Ferguson* is a compound of bad logic, bad history, bad sociology, and bad constitutional law. It ignored and ran counter to the history of the Civil Rights Act of 1866, the Freedmen's Bureau Act, the Fourteenth Amendment, and subsequent supplementary legislation, the firm purpose of all of which was to uproot unequal laws, customs, and traditions. It accepted uncritically either expressly or implicitly the vogue in social thinking in 1896 as reflected by theories of racial supremacy and social Darwinism. More important, it ran counter to the Court's own decisions from the Strauder case through the Civil Rights Cases. Restrictive as some of the Court's earlier decisions were with respect to the scope of the Fourteenth Amendment, they all emphatically condemned every legal distinction based on race or color and enunciated absolute equality before the law. Even the decision in the Civil Rights Cases is clear on this issue. Here the Court struck down an act of Congress abolishing segregation in public conveyances, inns, and theaters, on the ground that it was discrimination, not by the states, but by private action, and left the clear implication that segregation as a form of state discrimination would be unconstitutional as a denial of the equal protection of the laws and certainly within the power of Congress to condemn.

Moreover, the decisions in the Civil Rights Cases and in some of its predecessors, limiting the scope of equal protection were reached out of a tender solicitude for the maintenance of federalism. The decision in the Plessy case, although it sustained the validity of legislation, rested on laissez-faire assumptions with respect to governmental control of race relations. . . . Prior to the Plessy case the Court uniformly regarded all racial discrimination perpetrated by a state or its agencies as invidious and void regardless of its alleged reasonableness. On the basis of every consideration, therefore, the decision in the Plessy case was a departure from precedents and was wrong when made. Hence, when it was reversed fifty-eight years later, it should have been overturned on that ground and no other.

In contrast to the opinion of the Court, Justice Harlan's dissent was characterized by sound logic, accurate history as far as it went, correct constitutional law, and, above all these, high moral assumptions and aspirations. He rejected the idea that in the eyes of the Constitution and the laws there can be a superior, dominant, or ruling class, and proclaimed: "Our Constitution is color blind and neither knows nor tolerates classes among citizens. In respect of civil rights all citizens are equal before the law." With prophetic accuracy he forecast that the decision would "stimulate aggressions, more or less brutal and irritating," on the rights of Negroes and defeat the purposes of the Civil War amendments.

Although *Plessy* v. *Ferguson* was authoritative for fifty-eight years, and its rationale was extended to sustaining segregation in the public schools, subsequent judicial sanctions of it . . . are hardly impressive. Certainly, *Cumming* v. *Board of Education* was a frail support. There, all the Court did was to sustain the suspension of the sole Negro high school (containing sixty pupils) in a Georgia county so as to use its building for a Negro elementary school with three hundred pupils. Because three private high schools charging the same tuition fee as the Negro school were available to Negroes and because of the improper presentation of issues, Justice Harlan, as spokesman for a unanimous court, could find no evidence of racial discrimination. Moreover, the case did not in any way present the constitutional issue of segregated education. The same observations are true of *Gong Lum* v. *Rice,* in which Gong Lum, a Chinese, challenged only the classification of his daughter as colored so as to exclude her from white schools in the absence of separate schools for Chinese. It is true that Chief Justice William Howard Taft, as was often his habit, went beyond the necessities of the case to affirm the validity of segregated education on the basis of the Roberts and Plessy cases, and thereby continued the uncritical analogy between schools and transportation. Indeed, it was not until 1938 in *Missouri* ex rel. *Gaines* v. *Canada* that the equal but separate formula as applied to public education was given full acceptance by the Court, in a case directly presenting the issue. And this case, paradoxically, was the beginning of the end of racial segregation in the public schools. . . .

By 1900 the elaborate apparatus for the enforcement of equal rights in the Civil Rights Act of 1866, the Fourteenth and Fifteenth amendments, and subsequent legislation of 1870, 1871, and 1875 was largely a failure, . . . As the dour Thad Stevens had bitterly forecast, the day came when Democratic majorities in Congress, supported by a Democratic President, repealed substantial portions of the legislation. Even Republicans displayed a chronic indifference to racial discriminations except during election campaigns, when their interest became acute. Indifferent and inactive Presidents and disinterested or timid Attorneys General did little to enforce the amendments and the remnants of the statutes; and the Supreme Court, as we have seen, imposed very considerable obstacles by invalidating key provisions of federal statutes and construing others and the amendments strictly.

The net effect of all these cases was to make the Supreme Court, and not Congress, the major organ for the enforcement of the Fourteenth Amendment, contrary to the expectations of its framers and the clear meaning of its text. The transfer of power from Congress to the Court was a major constitutional defeat for the Radical Republicans, who were thereby deprived of the fruits of their political victories, and it was, in turn, a major triumph for the South, which was given a free hand in the control of race relations so long as southern states refrained from making or enforcing laws in an unequal, hostile, and oppressive manner. Although the South had lost the war, it had conquered constitutional law. Regardless of any subsequent developments in constitutional interpretation, the Court had emerged as an ally of the South in a most critical period of its existence as a conscious sectional minority. . . . It is melancholy to record that the southern states, instead of using their newly restored powers over race relations to bring about a gradual improvement of the legal, political, and economic status of Negroes, used them in a discriminatory and oppressive manner, with a view to keeping the colored race in a low, servile, and cringing status, under the leadership of irresponsible office seekers who fanned the flames of racial hatred and rode into office on the back of the Negro.

An authority on the historical background of the Fourteenth Amendment, ALFRED H. KELLY (b. 1907) is the author, along with Winfred A. Harbison, of a widely used textbook on American constitutional history, *The American Constitution: Its Origins and Development* (1970). Chairman of the Department of History at Wayne State University in Detroit, where he has taught for over twenty years, Kelly has been a prominent leader in civil rights scholarship. He was one of the scholar-experts summoned by General Counsel Thurgood Marshall (now an associate justice on the Supreme Court) to help prepare the NAACP brief on the origins of the Fourteenth Amendment in respect to segregation. In this essay, Kelly discusses the background of the 1930s and 1940s that culminated in the successful NAACP drive to overthrow the "separate but equal" doctrine.*

Alfred H. Kelly

The Coming of Brown *v.* Board of Education

On a certain warm and humid day in May, 1896, when the Supreme Court of the United States delivered its opinion in the Louisiana "Jim Crow" car case, entitled *Plessy* v. *Ferguson,* the American Negro stood at a kind of new nadir in his long struggle for decency and humanity. An overwhelming number of white Americans both North and South, the idealism of the Radical Republicans of a generation earlier now conveniently forgotten, rested secure in the comfortable assumption of the biological, cultural, and social superiority of the white race. . . .

It was to be a long road from *Plessy* . . . to that day in May, 1954, when Chief Justice Earl Warren, speaking for a unanimous Supreme Court, tossed the "separate but equal" rule into the rubbish heap of outworn constitutional doctrine. But just as in 1896, when Brown had spoken for a segregated America, the Supreme Court in 1954 was still adhering to its own larger rule: it was again "following the election returns." For in between *Plessy* and *Brown* v. *the Board of Education of the City of Topeka* there ensued a vast sociopolitical revolution in the status of the American Negro.

Seen in historical perspective, it is now apparent that this twentieth-century "revolution" in Negro status was to be no less far-reaching in its social and political consequences than that earlier revolution

*Abridged from pp. 244–269, "The School Desegregation Case," by Alfred H. Kelly in *Quarrels That Have Shaped the Constitution,* edited by John A. Garraty. Footnotes omitted.

in Negro status precipitated by the Civil War and Radical Republican Reconstruction. The "first Revolution," 1861–68, freed the Negro and endowed him with nominal citizenship and legal equality. Once the revolutionary tide had subsided, however, it left the ex-slave stranded. . . . The "second Revolution" in Negro status, which even today is far from complete, was to inaugurate the progressive destruction of the racial caste system in the United States and to commence at the same time the genuine integration of the Negro into the social, economic, and political fabric of American life.

The rise and progress of this vast new twentieth-century revolution in Negro status makes up too complex a story to be told in great detail here, but there can be no real grasp of the meaning of *Brown* v. *Board* without some understanding of it. Perhaps it is no great oversimplification to assert that it had its beginnings in the rise of numerically important and hence politically significant Negro communities in the many large and middle-sized cities of the American North, resulting in turn from successive waves of colored migration from the states of the Old Confederacy. Between 1910 and 1940, the Negro population of New York City, for example, rose from 60,000 to 450,000. . . . By 1940 twenty-six Northern cities had Negro populations of 10,000 or more.

The small Negro elite in these cities, composed of lawyers, doctors, schoolteachers, social workers, ministers, and the like, exercised a political influence all out of proportion to their numbers. They represented a community which even in the North was frightfully ghettoized and discriminated against economically, but which nonetheless had one all-important instrument of political power denied them in the South—the vote. Negro leaders used the votes they controlled to make alliances with local urban political machines, and so to win concessions for the Negro community. In Chicago, for example, Negroes were an important element in the political machine put together in the 1920's by William Hale Thompson and his henchmen. Negroes traded votes with Thompson for jobs on the city police force and the city hall bureaucracy, assurances of fair play for Negroes in the courts, access to a "fair share" of the city's bathing beaches, a lax attitude toward rent evictions, and so on. . . .

Negro political power of this kind in the 1920's was still essentially localized and without much influence on national political parties or national policy. However, the Great Depression and the New Deal nationalized the Negro's political significance in the great cities of the North by incorporating the colored voter as an essential ingredient in the new political machine which Franklin Roosevelt put together after 1933. The Negro suffered severely in the depression, and he came into the Roosevelt political combine with a new awareness of the significance of his political allegiance and a powerful determination to make the most of it. For the first time since Reconstruction, the Negro had a recognized position in a winning political combination of national scope.

The Negro's new political power revived almost immediately in the colored community an old, old dream—that of "first-class citizenship" in an integrated America. For two reasons, however, this dream found no very important political expression in the immediate postdepression period. First, the early New Deal had an overwhelming preoccupation with problems concerned with economic rehabilitation, a preoccupation which the Negro fully shared. . . .

Equally important in inhibiting any powerful New Deal drive for desegregation was the fact that Roosevelt's political combination rested upon a delicate balance between two exceedingly disparate parts: Northern urban political machines, including their politically powerful Negro component, and Southern white Democratic conservatives. . . . To these men any desegregation drive would have been anathema, and thus would have threatened party unity.

However, the World War II crisis worked another substantial acceleration in the growth of the Negro's national political power and influence. First, it created an unprecedentedly large demand for Negro labor in the great cities of the North. This not only produced a new wave of migration from the South which increased the voting power of the Northern urban community; it also forced the Negro into jobs, pay ratings, union memberships, and the like never open to him before. . . .

Second, the equalitarian ideology of American war propaganda, which presented the United States as a champion of democracy engaged in a death struggle with the German racists, created in the minds and hearts of most white persons a new and intense awareness of the shocking contrast between the country's too comfortable image of itself and the cold realities of American racial segregation. Both pragmatic propaganda interests and the new idealism demanded certain steps for the Negro's further integration, both in society and in the war effort.

Some of this crisis-imposed, wartime integration took place on an official level: in a series of executive orders, the Roosevelt administration expanded the employment of Negroes in the federal bureaucracy, wrote "no discrimination" clauses into war contracts, established in 1941 a Fair Employment Practices Commission, and even took a few hesitant steps toward racial integration in the armed forces. Meantime, in 1939, Attorney General Frank Murphy, already something of a radical idealist on the integration and Negro civil rights questions, had established a Civil Rights Division in the Department of Justice, which in turn undertook what was to prove to be a generation-long legal quest for new federal guarantees against lynching and new safeguards for Negro voting rights. . .

It was inevitable that the Negro's new nationalized political power, his enhanced economic position, and the vast improvement in ideological climate in the country presently would spill over into the courts, to produce a new series of decisions reflecting the altered position of the Negro in America. The dynamics of this process are hardly very mysterious. Several of the Roosevelt appointees to the Court after 1937 were practical politicians whom the exigencies of the New Deal had made intensely aware of the "political power shift" implicit in the Negro's new party role. Hugo Black, Robert Jackson, Frank Murphy, and Wiley Rutledge all fell into this category. Or, like Felix Frankfurter and William O. Douglas, the new appointees were legal academicians who reflected the equalitarian idealism of the liberal university communities of the North. . .

It needs only to be added here that the succession of justices appointed to the Court after the war—Fred M. Vinson, Harold Burton, Sherman Minton, and Tom Clark—while they tended generally to be more conservative than New Deal era justices, nonetheless had been trained in the hard practical school of politics and shared to the full an awareness of the altered position of the Negro in

American society. Earl Warren, the mild-mannered middle-of-the-road Republican who came to the chief justiceship in 1953, epitomized as no one else could have this new politico-judicial understanding. The Negro's altered role was no mere matter of New Deal radical idealism. It was a point of view which had been thoroughly absorbed by the working politicians of both parties.

It is hardly open to question, then, that this flow of Democratic and Republican appointees to the High Court after 1937 would in no great length of time have produced something of a constitutional revolution in the Negro's status. But this process, inevitable as it may well have been, was vastly accelerated by the legal assault on segregation first launched in the late 1930's by a powerful and dedicated Negro interest group, the National Association for the Advancement of Colored People. The desegregation campaign commenced about 1935 by the NAACP got under way very slowly, but it continued without interruption and with growing success for the next generation. It was a campaign which would make the NAACP the "cutting edge" of all the complex social and political forces that were at work to produce a desegregated America. . . .

The Association's early desegregation cases were under the general direction of Charles Houston, an Amherst Phi Beta Kappa, Harvard Law School graduate, and dean of the Howard University Law School. . . .

Destined to become by far the greatest legal asset of the Association, however, was Thurgood Marshall, a native of Baltimore, graduate of Lincoln University in Pennsylvania, and a product of Houston's training at the Howard Law School. Marshall, who joined the NAACP legal staff in the mid-thirties, brought to the Association a wonderfully keen and incisive mind, a sharp sense of legal strategy and political realities, and an ebullient spirit tempered both by a mordant sense of humor and a deep dedication to the Negro cause. In 1939, he became general counsel of the newly created NAACP Legal Defense and Education Fund, a unit technically divorced from the Association's propaganda and legislative activities. By 1950, Marshall, through the Legal Defense Fund, was directing the expenditure of some $150,000 annually in the prosecution of various desegregation cases throughout the country. So great was his success that the Negro community had come to know him as "Mr. Civil Rights."

There were a number of "fronts" in the Association's early legal campaign against segregation of which the attack on Jim Crow schools was only one. Others included suits against so-called "white primaries," against restrictive covenants in housing, and against Jim Crow transportation. The attack on white primaries, after some reverses, met success in 1944 when the Supreme Court ruled that such elections violated the Fourteenth Amendment. Prosecution directed against segregation in transportation also was very successful. Milestones came in *Mitchell* v. *United States* (1941), where the Supreme Court in effect ordered the desegregation of Pullman facilities; in *Morgan* v. *Virginia* (1945), in which the Court struck down state laws imposing racial segregation in interstate transportation facilities; and in *Henderson* v. *United States* (1950), in which the Court knocked out dining car segregation. This series of decisions was to be capped in 1955 by an Interstate Commerce Commission order directing the complete desegregation of all interstate transportation facilities in the country.

WOW

Of more ultimate significance for the *Brown* case was the Association's campaign to destroy restrictive racial covenants, in the course of which the NAACP developed a series of techniques which were to prove of great value in the campaign against school segregation. Of great importance was the resort to a series of regional and national lawyers' planning conferences, in which Marshall's New York office became a kind of "general staff headquarters," coordinating policy and strategy with the local attorneys handling such cases. The Association also engaged in extensive consultation with academic experts in economics, sociology, housing, and public administration, another technique which would prove to be of great value in fighting school segregation. . . . The climax of this carefully staged and well-coordinated campaign came in 1948, when the Supreme Court, in *Shelley* v. *Kraemer*, ruled that neighborhood racial covenants, while not in themselves unlawful, nonetheless could not be enforced in state courts, since such enforcement constituted state action in support of discrimination and hence violated the Fourteenth Amendment.

The Association's attack on segregated schools began in the middle thirties . . . a series of suits to force the admission of Negroes to Southern graduate professional schools, above all state university law schools. . . .

This "beachhead" strategy in the attack on school segregation started slowly enough, although it eventually yielded spectacular results. The first important victory came in 1938, when the Supreme Court ruled, in *Missouri ex rel Gaines* v. *Canada*, that refusal of a state university to admit a Negro to its law school, there being no comparable "separate but equal" institution available for Negroes, constituted a violation of the "equal protection" clause. Missouri, following a custom then common among Southern states, had offered to pay the prospective student's expenses to an unsegregated school in the North. But the Court refused to accept this device any longer. By Missouri's laws, Chief Justice Hughes's opinion pointed out, "a privilege has been created for white law students which is denied to Negroes." Sending the student to school in another state could not "remove the discrimination," which violated the Fourteenth Amendment.

The *Gaines* decision constituted, after all, only a very small breach in the wall of Southern segregation, and for some time no further advances occurred. . . .

Then at length, in 1948, in *Sipuel* v. *Board of Regents*, the Association's lawyers scored again, as the Supreme Court unanimously struck down an Oklahoma attempt to deny a Negro admission to the state university law school. Superficially, the decision resembled that in the *Gaines* case, but its significance became apparent when the Oklahoma Board of Regents soon thereafter voted, seven to one, to admit Negroes to any course of study not provided by the State College for Negroes. . . . "You can't build a cyclotron for one student," Oklahoma University President George L. Cross was said to have remarked at the time.

Two years later, in 1950, came Marshall's far more dramatic victory in *Sweatt* v. *Painter*, in which the Supreme Court spoiled a spectacular Texas attempt to turn the equal-protection question aside by setting up overnight a separate Negro law school. The plaintiff, a Houston mail carrier, had pressed an Association-backed suit in the state courts for admission to the law school of the University of Texas. But the State Supreme Court, instead of granting the request, had merely ordered the university to furnish Sweatt with "substantially equal" facilities for a legal education. Thereupon the university, in an atmosphere of intense controversy highlighted by faculty and student mass meetings on both sides of the question, "fitted out" a Negro law school and invited Sweatt to attend.

Sweatt, backed by Marshall and his colleagues, of course refused to oblige, and instead sued once more in the state courts for admission. Marshall now deliberately drew very heavily upon the techniques which the Association had matured in the covenant cases. A parade of legal and academic experts came to the stand, all of them carefully calculated to furnish testimony which would overwhelm the state's argument that the fly-by-night law school in question could in any real sense constitute substantial equality. . . . The Texas Supreme Court, setting testimony of this sort to one side, again ruled against Sweatt.

However, the Supreme Court of the United States on appeal ordered Sweatt's admission to the university's "white" law school. Chief Justice Vinson's opinion ridiculed the Texan claim that the state had managed to establish facilities for legal education that had any substantial equality, in faculty, library, or prestige. "It is difficult to believe," Vinson said, "that one who had a free choice between these law schools would consider the question close." . . .

McLaurin v. *Oklahoma Regents*, another Supreme Court decision handed down the same day as the *Sweatt* case, constituted an almost equally significant Association victory. Here the University of Oklahoma, compelled by suit to admit a Negro to its School of Education, had attempted to maintain segregation within the university itself by compelling the student to sit in a roped-off class section marked "reserved for colored," to use like reserved sections in the library and dining room, and so on. Unhesitatingly, the Court struck this practice down. Restrictions of this sort, Vinson's opinion said sternly, inevitably "handicapped" the student in his pursuit of "effective graduate instruction" and so violated the Fourteenth Amendment.

It was obvious to Marshall and his lieutenants that the *Sweatt* and *McLaurin* cases were of great significance, for they could be used to destroy racial segregation in graduate education virtually everywhere in the South. On the other hand, technically the Court had done nothing whatever to undermine the old *Plessy* "separate but equal rule." On the contrary, in one sense, at least, it had strengthened it, since in both cases it had held that the facilities in question were inadequate solely because they failed to meet the standard that the "separate but equal" rule required. . . . Indeed, all over the South, white boards of education, reading this implication into the *Sweatt* and *McLaurin* decisions, began crash programs of Negro school building, calculated, as Governor Byrnes of South Carolina presently frankly confessed, "to remedy a hundred years of neglect" of Negro education, lest the Supreme Court "take matters out of the state's hands."

Marshall later admitted that the NAACP was at this point at a kind of crossroads. The legal gap between the *Sweatt* and *McLaurin* cases on the one hand and an outright destruction of the *Plessy* precedent appeared to be appallingly wide, and he and his colleagues were not at all sure they could cross it. Might it not be well to "go along" with the Southern procedure, at least in part?

At this stage of the game, Marshall later told the author, if the school boards in key Southern states had shown a general disposition to accept any kind of gradualist program combining more adequate schools with some primary and secondary desegregation, the Association might well have agreed to cooperate, at least for a time.

Instead, school boards in South Carolina and in Virginia's Prince Edward County, both critical areas in the Association's planning, rejected outright all overtures for a gradualist program. "Sometimes history takes things into its own hands," Marshall said later, indicating that in his opinion Southern intransigence literally drove the NAACP to wage all-out war in the courts on segregated schools at every level.

Following a national conference on strategy in New York in September, 1950, Marshall and his staff commenced the prosecution of five segregation suits, at carefully selected points around the country. In Topeka, Kansas; in Clarendon County, South Carolina; and in Prince Edward County, Virginia, the Association filed suits in equity in federal district courts, in the name of local Negro schoolchildren, demanding their admission to "white" schools. These suits charged not only that local Negro schools were inferior to their white counterparts, but also that the "separate but equal" rule itself violated the equal-protection clause of the Fourteenth Amendment. Another suit commenced in the Chancery Court of the State of Delaware made substantially the same demands. A fifth action, begun in the District of Columbia, charged that segregation in the nation's capital violated the due-process clause of the Fifth Amendment, the same constitutional provision which Chief Justice Taney, nearly a hundred years earlier, had drawn on in the *Dred Scott* case to rule that Negro slavery could not be barred from any federal territory.

As Marshall had calculated in advance, these cases at the outset encountered substantial failure. . . .

All this, of course, amounted to little more than preliminary legal sparring. During the course of 1952, the Supreme Court granted reviews in all five of the foregoing cases, and in December the Court heard arguments from both sides. Marshall . . . and the other NAACP lawyers involved contended that *Plessy* v. *Ferguson* had been erroneously decided and was in any event obsolete, while Edward T. McGranahan, President Truman's Attorney General, also filed a brief as *amicus curiae* asking the Court to declare school segregation invalid under the equal-protection clause. In addition, in an appendix to the Association's brief, thirty social scientists of national reputation . . . not only attacked school segregation as possible in fact "only insofar as it is combined with discrimination" against the Negro child, but also argued at length that segregation did vast psychic damage both to Negro and white children. In turn, John W. Davis, distinguished constitutional lawyer and former Democratic Presidential candidate of 1924, presented a "powerful and effective" argument in defense of segregation for the school boards.

In June, 1953, after a six-month silence, the Supreme Court spoke. Instead of handing down a simple "yes" or "no" decision, however, the justices set the case for reargument, and asked counsel to prepare answers to a series of historical questions the justices now propounded, most of them having to do with the original intent of the framers of the Fourteenth Amendment with respect to school segregation. . . .

The very nature of these queries made it evident that the NAACP already had scored a significant victory. In a sense, the Court already had "taken sides," in that it had at long last consented to re-examine the question of the Fourteenth Amendment's "original" meaning. The implication in the very raising of such a question was obvious enough. The Court intended to destroy the "separate but equal" rule if it could discover a plausible rationale for doing so. The justices, in fact, seemed virtually to be saying something like the following to the NAACP lawyers: "Provide us, if you can, with some plausible historical argument which will relieve us of undue embarrassment and we will only too gladly set the 'separate but equal' rule aside."

Here was opportunity—magnificent opportunity, as Marshall and his fellows recognized—but it was opportunity hedged about with evident danger. The Association lawyers were not historians, and they had no idea of what a careful examination of the evidence might reveal. The debates in the *Congressional Globe* for 1866 might not reveal the framers' intent with respect to school segregation. Worse yet, investigation of the historical record might even provide the proponents of segregation with historical arguments so decisive that the Court would feel itself obliged to confirm the *Plessy* rule. As Marshall put it later, what looked like a "golden gate" might "turn out to be a booby trap with a bomb in it."

Confronted with this touchy problem, Marshall decided to turn once more to the academic world for assistance—a step he would later characterize as "the smartest move I ever made in my life." He called an NAACP conference to meet in New York in late September, and issued invitations to some 130 social scientists, most of them American historians and constitutional experts. At the same time, he sought out and commissioned several historians to prepare research papers on various aspects of the questions the Court had posed. Howard J. Graham of Los Angeles and the present author, both constitutional historians, prepared monographs on the passage and ratification of the Fourteenth Amendment . . . Repeatedly, during the planning of the NAACP case, Marshall had told his advisers that they did not need to *win* the historical argument. All that was required was a face-saving draw. "A nothin'-to-nothin' score," he said with typical directness, "means we win the ball game." . . .

On December 8, a Supreme Court chamber filled to overflowing heard Marshall and Spottswood Robinson argue that the framers of the Fourteenth Amendment had intended to ban segregation "as a last vestige of slavery." John W. Davis, presenting oral arguments for the respondents, asserted in reply with equal confidence and force that "it is not within the judicial power" for the Court to set aside, merely "on a sociological basis," a school system that "has stood for three-quarters of a century."

The justices themselves interrupted from time to time to ask an occasional searching question. Frankfurter rather pointedly inquired of Marshall whether, if the Southern states now were to agree to spend money for "more and better schools for Negroes," he would still insist that segregation was unconstitutional. Needless to say, the Justice got a strongly affirmative answer. And Douglas asked Solicitor General J. Lee Rankin, who presented the government's brief, whether the Court properly could decide the present cases "either way." No, Rankin insisted, the Court "properly could find only one answer."

The Court's decision, handed down on May 17, 1954, after another long silence, could hardly have occasioned any great surprise either to the proponents or enemies of segregated schools. Chief Justice Warren's opinion for a unanimous Court was remarkable both for its simplicity and for the extraordinary fashion in which it avoided all legal and historical complexities. The historical question of intent which had occasioned both sides so much anxiety he pushed aside almost impatiently as impossible of resolution. But in the light of conditions in the twentieth century, he said, it was obvious that enforced segregation generated "a feeling of inferiority" in Negro children which might well inflict such grave damage to their minds and hearts that it could never be undone. Public school segregation by state law, therefore, violated the equal-protection clause of the Fourteenth Amendment; the old *Plessy* "separate but equal" rule, he added, was herewith formally overruled.

Thus the NAACP came to its greatest triumph—a landmark decision destroying completely the constitutional foundations upon which legalized segregation in the South rested.

It was the end of a long road, yet in another sense only a beginning. For the justices did not order immediate desegregation of Southern schools in the 1954 opinion; instead, in a subsidiary decision a year later, the Court invoked a principle from equity law to order desegregation carried out under local federal court direction "with all deliberate speed."

Thus the justices carefully separated the delineation of the principle of integration from the actual implementation thereof. At the same time they avoided very nicely the crisis they would have produced had they ordered *immediate* desegregation. And one can speculate that this very careful separation of principle from implementation was one reason why the Court was able to present a united front to the world in its 1954 decision.

Yet for all its cautious self-limitation, the Court's decision in *Brown* v. *Board* remains one of the great landmarks in the history of American liberty. In a sense, the Court was "legislating," for, sweeping aside state decisions and decisions based on mere law and precedent, it vested its opinion on broad considerations of national welfare. Thus the decision was indeed "political" in the deepest sense of the word, as the Court's enemies charged. Yet the fact is that the Court's greatest decisions have always been political, for unless we subscribe to the notion of a completely static Constitution and a "slot machine" theory of constitutional law, the Court must perforce decide questions of the kind it faced in *Brown* in a "political" fashion.

EDMOND CAHN (1906–1964) was for many years professor of law at the New York University School of Law. Aside from his involvement in constitutional and legal analysis, Cahn was much concerned with the relationship of moral philosophy to law. His books include *The Sense of Injustice* (1949), *The Predicament of Democratic Man* (1961), and two edited works, *Supreme Court and Supreme Law* (1954) and *The Great Rights* (1963). The excerpt below is from one of his periodic commentaries on recent issues in jurisprudence. It is interesting that Cahn's skepticism toward social science evidence in the *Brown* case was used primarily by opponents of the decision in their attempts to discredit it. But Cahn was sure the *School Segregation* cases rested on solid moral and constitutional ground. For his detailed critique of the weakness of the social science evidence, see the original article in full.*

Edmond Cahn

The School Cases: Based on Moral Values, Not Social Science

In legal philosophy it is a very dangerous thing to comment on happenings that one welcomes and approves. By doing so, an unwary observer may expose himself to the occupational disease of jurisprudence, which in its most virulent form consists in finding the law "the true embodiment of everything that's excellent." When the disease takes hold, its victim gradually loses his early vigor of discontent and passion for reform; by slow stages he subsides into a state of complacency; in course of time, sitting at ease among his memories, he grows to resent the process of change as ardently as he used to welcome it. . . . The risk is a dire one. Nevertheless, in the teeth of the danger, I shall proceed to comment here on 1954's most important development: the Supreme Court's decisions in the *School Segregation* cases. When the sense of injustice has triumphed on a scale so extensive, comprehension of the meaning of victory may prove useful to it in other conflicts. The decisions have added to the dignity and stature of every American.

There is no need to speculate on the Supreme Court's unanimity in *Brown* v.

---

* Edmond Cahn, "Jurisprudence," *New York University Law Review*, 30 (January 1955), 150–160, 167–169. Reprinted with permission of the *New York University Law Review* and Mrs. Edmond Cahn. Footnotes omitted.

Board of Education and *Bolling* v. *Sharpe*.* Before the opinions were announced, there may have been considerable room for doubt concerning their purport, but, at least in the eyes of sophisticated observers, there was hardly any question that the court would be unanimous or nearly unanimous. The train of previous decisions dealing with the same subject matter had long since established this institutional policy.

Chief Justice Warren's style in the *Brown* and *Bolling* opinions is most commendably bland. Very wisely he declined the opportunity—one may say, the temptation—to indulge in democratic rhetoric. There is not a word of reproach or provocation in either opinion. To his credit, the Chief Justice was less concerned with getting into the anthologies than with presenting the country with a model of rational calm. . . .

Among the many interesting aspects of these opinions, the Court's mode of interpreting the Fourteenth Amendment deserves very special attention. Never was Thomas Jefferson more clearly vindicated in his insistence that the Constitution belongs to the living generation of Americans. The question has become: What do the phrases mean here and now? The meaning of the Amendment is to be found in the relation of its language to a total haecceity, including everything that has changed and everything we have learned and unlearned since 1868 when it was adopted. There were two lines of history for the Court to evaluate. The first of them—the history of the framing and adopting of the Fourteenth Amendment—proved to be only a casual element in the social and constitutional complex, an element far too ambiguous to be considered very important, much less decisive.

This was demonstrated rather adroitly. In an order for reargument, the Justices requested the parties to dredge up whatever they could to show what the men of post-Civil War days had had in view concerning public education; zealously the various parties complied; after heavy labors, they adduced evidence as contradictory, amorphous, and confused as might have been—and, I suspect, was—anticipated; whereupon the Court, with little show of disappointment, turned brusquely away from the mind of the nineteenth century and proceeded to put the mind of the twentieth century to work. The historical data continue to make interesting matter for reading, and not much more. Meanwhile, the order for reargument had hinted the outcome of the cases broadly enough to remove any resentment based on mere surprise.

Turning from history of the amendment to history of the development of public education, the Court provided itself with much more consistent and objective indicia. One can see rather clearly the progression from what public education had been in 1868, when the amendment was adopted, to 1896, when *Plessy* v. *Ferguson* was decided, and on to what it has become in our time. In view of this enormous growth, the Chief Justice rightly emphasized the new and paramount significance of free education in the political and cultural life of mid-twentieth century America. Surely then, the past cannot be allowed to decide for us what it did not have to decide for itself. . . .

* *Bolling* v. *Sharpe* made applicable for the federal government in the District of Columbia the same standard of desegregated schools as the *Brown* opinion applied to the states.—Ed.

Occasionally everyone meets with an argument which he feels unworthy of the compliment of rational refutation. In

1920 Amend after 1954

defense of racial segregation many such arguments have been advanced, enough in fact to create a danger that judgment and analysis may be entirely suspended and, instead of a reasoned debate, a blind struggle of wills may eventuate. Fortunately, since time is on the side of those who insist on desegregation, they can afford to keep their heads without weakening their cause, which those who stand for the old order cannot.

For example there is the argument that it would be fruitless to end segregation in the schools because "voluntary" segregation will continue in the social community. It is hard to dignify this proposition by discussing it. . . . When imposed by the government, segregation constitutes an official disparagement of the Negro group. The disparagement is the crueler because, the United States being a political democracy, the government's implied judgment that Negroes are inferior is imputable to the entire citizenry. On the other hand, as the recent experience of the Armed Forces has demonstrated, when desegregation is effected under official auspices, both groups benefit from the lesson in decency and fair dealing.

But there are limits—even to the just claims of a political democracy. It would be ridiculous to contend that every citizen ought to select his or her social companions from a proportionate cross-section of the ethnic groups that make up the American people. If there is any area in which personal tastes, affinities, and irrational preferences may healthfully govern our behavior, it is in the process of selecting our social companions. When we resolve to observe the principles of the Constitution in every activity that is sponsored or controlled by government, our ability to do so in a willing and congenial manner may well depend on our being free, spontaneous, and unhampered in the remainder of our relationships. Somehow, sometime people will consort with whom they choose. For this reason, the distinction between official and unofficial segregation—a distinction to which the Supreme Court has adhered consistently—seems indispensable to furthering harmony among diverse racial groups. Discrimination in regard to corporate advantages (such as transportation, housing, employment, political franchise, or educational opportunity) violates the American promise; but discrimination in the choice of friends and private associates may furnish the very safety valve that many Americans require for psychic health. . . .

Here we see again the falseness of the widespread popular belief that, with regard to moral values, the law imposes only "minimum standards." While there are some fields in which this belief may be warranted, it becomes baseless when we enter the area of the Bill of Rights and the Fourteenth Amendment. Far from being merely "minimum standards," the substantive and procedural requirements of the Bill of Rights are so high that virtually no citizen lives up to them consistently in his personal relations and transactions. In the forum of conscience and private judgment, due process is violated continually by every one of us, including the lawyers and jurists who seek most earnestly to impose it on official action. Thus while the *Brown* and *Bolling* cases make us sensible of improvement in government performance, they do raise some disquieting questions concerning our behavior in the realm of the domestic and unofficial.

The decisions likewise cast a revealing light on the institution of judicial review. Since as a practical matter it would have been impossible to secure adoption of a constitutional amendment to abolish "separate but equal," only the Court possessed effective power to relieve American education of the incubus. It was to be court action or an impasse, and an impasse could not last indefinitely. For decades the public sense of injustice had denounced racial discrimination more and more resentfully. I suggest therefore that the *Brown* and *Bolling* decisions spared the nation a genuine constitutional crisis, and that in this exigency the institution of judicial review rendered an invaluable service.

In the Virginia case and to a lesser extent in the other litigations, various psychiatrists, psychologists, and social scientists gave expert testimony concerning the harmful effects of segregation on Negro school children. In addition, some of appellants' witnesses prepared an elaborate statement on the subject, which, signed by a total of thirty-two experts, was submitted to the Supreme Court as an appendix to appellants' brief. In the months since the utterance of the *Brown* and *Bolling* opinions, the impression has grown that the outcome, either entirely or in major part, was caused by the testimony and opinions of the scientists, and a genuine danger has arisen that even lawyers and judges may begin to entertain this belief. The word "danger" is used advisedly, because I would not have the constitutional rights of Negroes—or of other Americans—rest on any such flimsy foundation as some of the scientific demonstrations in these records.

The moral factors involved in racial segregation are not new—like the science of social psychology—but exceedingly ancient. What, after all, is the most elementary and conspicuous fact about a primitive community if not the physical proximity of human beings mingling together? When the members of a community decide to exclude one of their number from the group life without killing him outright, what else can they do but force him to remove himself physically (as in the case of Cain), ostracize him for what they consider the general welfare (as the Athenians did), banish him from the cluster of community dwellings (as in outbreaks of leprosy or other plague), assign him a fixed area or ghetto to occupy (as with the Jews in medieval times), or lock him in a penitentiary (as we do with convicted criminals)? Hardly anyone has been hypocritical enough to contend that no stigma or loss of status attaches to these forms of physical separation. Segregation does involve stigma; the community knows it does. . . .

There are people who argue, sometimes quite sincerely, that racial segregation is not *intended* to humiliate or stigmatize. On first impression, the argument seems to have some slight mitigative value, for surely a deliberate insult is liable to cut deeper than one inflicted out of mere crudeness or insensibility. But the mitigation comes too late. An excuse that one did not intend to injure does not stand much chance of reception when the offender, having been informed of the damage he has done, continues and persists in the same old callous insults. . . .

Moreover, if affronts are repeated often enough, they may ultimately injure the victim's backbone. We hear there are American Negroes who protest they do not feel insulted by racially segregated public schools. If there are any such Negroes, then they are the ones who have been injured most grievously of all, because segregation has shattered their spines and deprived them of self-respect.

So one speaks in terms of the most familiar and universally accepted standards of right and wrong when one remarks (1) that racial segregation under government auspices inevitably inflicts humiliation, and (2) that official humiliation of innocent, law-abiding citizens is psychologically injurious and morally evil. Mr. Justice Harlan and many other Americans with responsive consciences recognized these simple, elementary propositions before, during, and after the rise of "separate but equal." For at least twenty years, hardly any cultivated person has questioned that segregation is cruel to Negro school children. The cruelty is obvious and evident. Fortunately, it is so very obvious that the Justices of the Supreme Court could see it and act on it even after reading the labored attempts by plaintiffs' experts to demonstrate it "scientifically."

. . . When scientists set out to prove a fact that most of mankind already acknowledges, they may provide a rather bizarre spectacle. Fifty years ago, certain biologists who were engaged in just this sort of enterprise, provoked George Bernard Shaw to denounce their "solemnly offering us as epoch-making discoveries their demonstrations that dogs get weaker and die if you give them no food; that intense pain makes mice sweat; and that if you cut off a dog's leg the three-legged dog will have a four-legged puppy." Then Mr. Shaw called the scientists a number of fearful names (beginning with "dolts" and "blackguards"), none of which would be remotely applicable to the psychologists and psychiatrists who testified in the desegregation cases. So far as I can judge, all of these are fine, intelligent, dedicated scholars. Yet one can honor them as they deserve without swallowing their claims.

Professor Kenneth B. Clark of the psychology department of City College acted as general social science consultant to the NAACP legal staff and served as liaison between the lawyers and the scientists. His endeavors having been long and arduous, perhaps it was natural that he should exaggerate whatever the experts contributed to the case. In an article written while the country was waiting for the Supreme Court's decisions, he asserted, "*Proof* of the arguments that segregation itself is inequality and that state imposed racial segregation inflicts injuries upon the Negro *had to come from the social psychologists and other social scientists.* (Emphasis supplied.)

When Professor Clark wrote thus, he could not know that Chief Justice Warren's opinions would not mention either the testimony of the expert witnesses or the submitted statement of the thirty-two scientists. The Chief Justice cushioned the blow to some extent by citing certain professional publications of the psychological experts in a footnote, alluding to them graciously as "modern authority." In view of their devoted efforts to defeat segregation, this was the kind of gesture a magnanimous judge would feel impelled to make, and we are bound to take satisfaction in the accolade. Yet, once the courtesy had been paid, the Court was not disposed in the least to go farther or base its determination on the expert testimony. . . .

Obviously, the *Brown* and *Bolling* opinions are susceptible of more than one interpretation. My views do not agree with those of some very able commentators, who consider that the opinions show important marks of the psychologists' influence. Granting this variety of interpretations, does it really matter whether the Supreme Court relies or does not rely on the psychologists' findings? Does it make any practical difference?

I submit it does. In the first place, since the behavioral sciences are so very young, imprecise, and changeful, their findings have an uncertain expectancy of life. Today's sanguine asseveration may be cancelled by tomorrow's new revelation—or new technical fad. It is one thing to use the current scientific findings, however ephemeral they may be, in order to ascertain whether the legislature has acted reasonably in adopting some scheme of social or economic regulation; deference here is shown not so much to the findings as to the legislature. It would be quite another thing to have our fundamental rights rise, fall, or change along with the latest fashions of psychological literature. Today the social psychologists—at least the leaders of the discipline—are liberal and egalitarian in basic approach. Suppose, a generation hence, some of their successors were to revert to the ethnic mysticism of the very recent past; suppose they were to present us with a collection of racist notions and label them "science." What then would be the state of our constitutional rights? Recognizing as we do how sagacious Mr. Justice Holmes was to insist that the Constitution be not tied to the wheels of any economic system whatsoever, we ought to keep it similarly uncommitted in relation to the other social sciences.

There is another potential danger here. It concerns the guarantee of "equal protection of the laws." Heretofore, no government official has contended that he could deny equal protection with impunity unless the complaining parties offered competent proof that they would sustain or had sustained some permanent (psychological or other kind of) damage. The right to equal protection has not been subjected to any such proviso. Under my reading of the *Brown* and *Bolling* opinions, this would remain the law. But if, in future "equal protection" cases, the Court were to hold that it was the expert testimony that determined the outcome of *Brown* and *Bolling,* the scope of the constitutional safeguard might be seriously restricted. Without cataloguing the various possibilities, one can discern at least that some of them would be ominous. It is not too soon to say so, for basic rights need early alarms.

When the American people suffered a moral defeat in *Plessy* v. *Ferguson,* Mr. Justice Harlan's dissent survived on the record. It reminded the people of the solemn promises and mutual pledges that had inspired their beginnings as a nation, and appealed from what was narrow and mean in their traditions to what was broad and fraternal. As years went by Harlan's prophetic phrases were taken up, repeated, and reiterated—until they passed gradually into the popular vocabulary. Clergymen, social scientists, publicists, and jurists imagined they were coining novel phrases as they unwittingly borrowed his, which he would have been glad to lend them. By the end of the 1930s, when the Supreme Court began to utter its series of lessons to the states on fair treatment in education, the American people were fully prepared to support their judicial pedagogue. Now the advance has reached its climax, with the principle of equality firmly established. In this struggle, there can be no one to hail as victor except the whole American people, who alone have the power to insure that the principle becomes a living reality in their public schools. The achievement is theirs. With this, I believe, the lone dissenter of 1896 would agree. Even as the shame of his time belonged to all, so should the vindication of our time; and so too the hope of a more benevolent American community.

At the time the *Brown* case was decided, EUGENE COOK (1904–1967) was attorney general of Georgia, a position he had held since 1945. From 1965 to 1967 Cook served as a justice on the Georgia Supreme Court. WILLIAM I. POTTER (1888–1968) received both his undergraduate and legal education at the University of Missouri and was a prominent member of the Kansas City, Missouri, bar. Their joint article opposing the *Brown* decision appeared in the *American Bar Association Journal* and was paired with an article favoring the decision. Note that Cook and Potter refer to Cahn's article to support their attack on the Court's opinion. Their critique of *Brown* ranges widely, but what seems to be the heart of their objections?*

Eugene Cook
William I. Potter

The Court Overstepped Its Role

The purpose of this article is to discuss without heat and, it is hoped, with some light, from a strictly legal, and not emotional, viewpoint the precedent-shattering decisions of the Supreme Court in the school segregation cases of 1954 and 1955.

The decisions of the United States Supreme Court of May 17, 1954, and May 31, 1955, in the school segregation cases, *Brown* v. *Board of Education* . . . constitute a crisis in American constitutional law, for these reasons:

1. They are a radical departure from the doctrine of *stare decisis* firmly established in American and English jurisprudence. Moreover, the Court, as hereinafter pointed out, sustains its conclusion by a reasoning process which was heretofore unknown to jurisprudence, which conflicts with prior opinions of the same Court less than five years old, and which is sharply deprecated even by those who otherwise approve the result of the decision. If the reasoning by which the Court arrives at its conclusion is fatally defective, is not the result itself fatally defective?

2. The Court has, without any implementing act of the Congress such as is required under the terms of the Fourteenth Amendment, and by an order unprecedented in judicial history, assumed the power under that Amendment

* Eugene Cook and William I. Potter, "The School Segregation Cases; Opposing the Opinion of the Supreme Court," *American Bar Association Journal,* 42 (April 1956), 313–317, 391. Reprinted with permission. Copyright by the American Bar Association. Footnotes omitted.

to enforce commingling of the white and colored races in state-supported schools, thus rendering a nullity state laws providing for separate but equal educational facilities—an anomalous assumption of power that constitutes further encroachment by the central Government upon the rights reserved to the states and to the people by the Federal Constitution.

3. In construing segregated schools as unconstitutional and discriminatory against the Negro by reason of the equal protection clause of the Fourteenth Amendment, the Court reached the conclusion that the Negro was deprived of equal protection because the segregated school generated in him a feeling of inferiority that *may* (italics supplied) affect his heart and mind in a way *unlikely* (italics supplied) ever to be undone. To support this thesis it cited as authority college professors, psychologists and sociologists. Absent from the opinion was reference to the effect on the hearts and minds of white children and their parents because of enforced commingling with Negro children. The state, in providing segregated schools, gave heed to this preference of white parents and their children, and, desiring that state maintained free public schools should exist to educate the children of both races, solved this basic human problem by enacting laws and providing for equal educational facilities in separate schools. Reason supports the soundness and fairness of the state program, and reason supports prior decisions of the United States Supreme Court since the adoption of the Fourteenth Amendment in 1868, upholding the constitutionality of state-maintained separate-but-equal educational facilities.

The first point the Court had to resolve in the *Brown* case was whether the framers and ratifiers of the Fourteenth Amendment intended the equal protection clause to abolish segregation in the public schools. To this question the Supreme Court pleaded ignorance by saying that the intent of the framers and ratifiers "cannot be determined with any degree of certainty."

The Court said this, even though the briefs show that the same 39th Congress that promulgated the Fourteenth Amendment passed two bills dealing with separate schools for white and colored children in the District of Columbia. In addition, the briefs show that of the thirty-seven states in existence at that time, only five abolished segregation contemporaneously with ratification of the Fourteenth Amendment, and three of these restored segregation after the removal of federal troops.

The overwhelming majority either established or continued segregation in their public schools contemporaneously with ratification of the Fourteenth Amendment. Georgia's first public school segregation laws were enacted at the same session at which the Fourteenth Amendment was ratified. They were enacted by a Republican legislature which had thirty-three Negro members and were signed by a Republican governor. . . .

In rendering its decision, the Supreme Court rejected the traditional rule of constitutional construction and substituted the intent of the Court for the intent of the people.

In its article entitled "The Supreme Court 1953 Terms," the *Harvard Law Review* (68 *Harv. L. Rev.* 96) said:

> In dealing with prior cases, especially *Plessy* v. *Ferguson,* the Chief Justice did not seek to demonstrate that the court had once blundered. His point, rather, was that these prior decisions were simply outmoded in present day society.

Thus, it is seen that a new rule of testing the constitutionality of a state's public policy as expressed in its statutes and as authorized by the Tenth Amendment has been formulated. No longer is there a question of whether there exists a conflict with precedent or whether precedent is wrong but rather whether the intent of the framers as recognized in previous decisions, is, in the opinion of the Judges, "outmoded."

The purpose of all sincere investigations is the discovery of truth. Basic truth is discoverable in the midst of external realities. It may not be manufactured by the mind. It is a tangible reality and is never new. Once found, we may seize and hold fast to it. Now let us seek and follow the truth wherever it may lead, as applied to the *Brown* case.

In its decision, the Supreme Court did not hold that the old "separate but equal" doctrine, laid down in *Plessy* v. *Ferguson* . . . was bad law. It held that it was bad sociology. It did not hold that the facts (or truths) disclosed by the records in the cases before the Court, justified a departure from the "separate but equal" doctrine. It held that "psychological knowledge," apart from these records, was of more validity than factual truths.

Without doubt there is no precedent in any recorded decision of any court, and it is hoped there will be none hereafter, reading as follows: "Whatever may have been the extent of psychological knowledge at the time of *Plessy* v. *Ferguson,* this finding is amply supported by modern authority." (Citing as authority six lay textbooks, not introduced in evidence in any of the pending cases, clearly inadmissible if offered, and written, for the most part, by authors to whose affiliations and convictions the Court cannot have given the slightest investigation or attention, but which will hereafter be discussed in this article). . . .

How did such "intangibles" become "findings" in these cases? They were not authenticated as "authority" by any method known to Anglo-Saxon jurisprudence or rules of evidence. If not in evidence, the universal rule is that it was harmful error, prejudicial to the parties defendant, for them to be considered by the Court.

We have scanned legal literature since May, 1954, in an effort to find a respectable vindication of the Supreme Court's conduct, but have found none that appeals to reason.

Under elementary and elemental law, a court may not consider treatises in a field other than law, unless the treatises themselves are the very subject of inquiry. The doctrine of judicial notice extends only to those things of common knowledge that lie without the realm of science, or to that one science in which judges are presumed to be learned or experts themselves—the science of law. . . .

The findings of social science are sometimes regarded as elaborate statements of what everybody knows in language that nobody can understand. While little harm can come from such an undertaking, great harm will result when a social scientist takes his deductions and generalizations into the field of judicial interpretation and treats them as the equivalent of "law."

United States Circuit Judge Jerome Frank recently wrote that these generalizations and the "inferences derived therefrom are almost certain to be importantly false. For the consequences of the operation of certain customs or group attitudes are often cancelled out by the consequences of other conflicting customs and attitudes."

Even the latest book cited by the Court itself in footnote 11 of the *Brown* case (Witmer and Kotinsky) states:

> Unfortunately for scientific accuracy and adequacy, thoroughly satisfactory methods of determining the effects of prejudice and discrimination on health or personality have not yet been devised, nor has a sufficient number of studies dealing with the various minority groups been made.

But the Court blandly and extra-judicially accepts as "psychological *knowledge*" what the lay experts themselves are as yet completely unsure of!

Indeed, even stronger views have been expressed of the present wholly inadequate and unscientific state of sociological knowledge of majority-minority problems.

A recent writer, Edmond Cahn, who agrees with the result of the *Brown* case nevertheless sharply criticizes the use of sociological authority and shows its danger by saying:

> The word "danger" is used advisedly, because I would not have the constitutional rights of Negroes—or of other Americans—rest on such flimsy foundations as some of the scientific demonstrations in these records.

Since these behavioral sciences are so very young, imprecise and changeable, their findings have an uncertain expectancy of life. Today's observation may be cancelled by tomorrow's new revelation—or new technical fad.

Should our fundamental rights rise, fall or change along with the latest fashions of psychological literature? How are we to know that in the future social scientists may not present us with a collection of notions similar to those of Adolf Hitler and label them as modern science? If Mr. Justice Holmes was correct when he insisted that the Constitution should not be tied to the wheels of any economic system whatsoever, shouldn't it be similarly uncommitted in relation to other social sciences?

What of this modern authority upon which the Court based its decision?

The first one cited of the six—K. B. Clark—was, at the time of the arguments before the Court, on the payroll of the National Association for the Advancement of Colored People as a so-called "social-science expert," a questionable procedure in view of the fact that the NAACP was the real party in interest waging the litigation in these cases.

The book *An American Dilemma,* written by Swedish socialist Gunnar Myrdal on a grant from the Carnegie Foundation, was cited in its entirety by the Supreme Court as an authority for its ruling.

A contributor to this work was Negro educator W. E. B. DuBois, who sent a message of condolence upon the death of Joseph Stalin.

It was *in this book* that Myrdal declared the United States Constitution to be "impractical and unsuited to modern conditions" and its adoption to be "nearly a plot against the common people." Furthermore, he openly avowed that liberty must be forsaken for the benefit of what he called "social equality."

Has the present Supreme Court now adopted Myrdal's view of the Constitution? In all fairness have not we Southerners good reason to be deeply disturbed over the Court's attitude toward the Constitution? Has not every citizen good reason to be deeply disturbed? . . .

It is our firm opinion that the United States Supreme Court in *Brown* v. *Topeka* not only usurped the prerogatives of the people by amending the Federal Constitution in violation of Article V relating to amendment, but it pursued its pseudo-socio-psychological pattern by usurping the prerogatives of the United States Congress. It handed down an implementation decision on May 31, 1955, in spite of the fact that the Fourteenth Amendment itself vests in Congress the power of implementation.

The fifth section of the Fourteenth Amendment itself declares that "Congress shall have the power to enforce by appropriate legislation the provisions of this article." . . .

Title 42. Sections 1751–60 U.S.C.A., which, providing for a school lunch program by the Department of Agriculture for public and non-profit schools, provides: "If a state maintains separate schools for minority and majority races, no funds made available pursuant to this chapter shall be paid or disbursed to it unless a just and equitable distribution is made within the state, for the benefit of such minority races, of funds paid to it under this chapter."

Since the Congress has not, pursuant to its power under Section 5 of the Fourteenth Amendment, attempted to prohibit the maintenance by the states of segregated schools, but has impliedly by the enactment of said Sections 1751–60, Title 42 U.S.C.A., aforementioned, approved them, it is apparent that the present Supreme Court has overruled both the Congress and the will of the people as expressed in state constitutions and laws. . . . Moreover, the acts of Congress, Title 8, Section 1151 U.S.C.A., setting up the quota system of immigration which practically excludes immigration to the United States from geographical areas containing Negroes and Mongolians, were justified by reason of the fact that such races are not readily assimilated into the predominantly white, Caucasian race here. Such is a sound and necessary public policy to preserve the essentially Western civilization in the Continental United States. Clearly, therefore, that long-established public policy of the Congress and of the states is sought to be overturned, without their consent by a strained construction of the equal protection clause of the Fourteenth Amendment. . . .

In its singlemindedness and preoccupation in seeking to justify a radically new construction of the equal protection clause of the Fourteenth Amendment so as to outlaw state segregated schools, it by-passed and overrode the much greater constitutional principles that the people are sovereign, that the national Government has only specific powers delegated to it by the Constitution, and that all other powers reside in the states and the people. The Court has thus dealt a vital blow to the very heart and framework of our constitutional republic, which fits in with the pattern set in recent years of encroachment by the executive and judicial departments upon the rights reserved to the states and to the people by the Constitution. When, by this process, the Constitution is finally completely whittled away without a vote of the people or consent of the states, the dreams envisioned by some of the authors cited by the Court are ready for attainment, and then comes death to liberty in America.

JAMES F. BYRNES (b. 1878) has a long career of high-level public service. A moderate southern Democrat on most issues, he was a member of the House from 1911–1925 and then Senator from 1931–1941, when he was appointed an associate justice of the Supreme Court. He left the Court in 1942 to become President Roosevelt's Director of Economic Stabilization during World War II. Later he was Director of War Mobilization. From 1945–1947 he was Secretary of State during the intensification of the Cold War. In 1951 he returned to South Carolina politics as governor and instituted a crash program to bring the segregated Negro schools up to par with the white schools. His article for the widely circulated *U.S. News & World Report,* calling for a "curb" on the Court, brought the prestige of his former associate justiceship to the growing attack on the Court. Byrnes' article covers a broad range of criticisms of the Court's decision, but what appears to be his most basic objection?*

James F. Byrnes

The Court Must Be Curbed

Two years ago, on May 17, 1954, the Supreme Court of the United States reversed what had been the law of the land for 75 years and declared unconstitutional the laws of 17 States under which segregated public-school systems were established.

The Court did not interpret the Constitution—the Court amended it.

We have had a written Constitution. Under that constitution the people of the United States have enjoyed great progress and freedom. The usurpation by the Court of the power to amend the Constitution and destroy State governments may impair our progress and take our freedom.

An immediate consequence of the segregation decision is that much of the progress made in the last half century of steadily advancing racial amity has been undone. Confidence and trust have been supplanted by suspicion and distrust. The races are divided and the breach is widening. The truth is, there has not been such tension between the races in the South since the days of Reconstruction.

One threatened consequence is the closing of public schools in many States of the South.

*Reprinted from *U.S. News & World Report,* May 18, 1956. James F. Byrnes, "The Supreme Court Must Be Curbed."

A further consequence is the harm done to the entire country by the demonstrated willingness of the Supreme Court to disregard our written Constitution and its own decisions, invalidate the laws of States, and substitute for these a policy of its own, supported not by legal precedents but by the writings of sociologists.

Today, this usurpation by the Court of the power of the States hurts the South. Tomorrow, it may hurt the North, East and West. It may hurt *you*.

Though there was no dissenting opinion from any member of the Court, the South dissents. That dissent is reflected in State legislation and in the day-by-day occurrences throughout the South, developments which portray the feeling of the people.

Only now do people living elsewhere begin to comprehend the determination behind the dissent of the South. Only now is an effort being made in the Northern press to give thoughtful, balanced and reasonably impartial presentation of what might be called "the Southern point of view."

The suppression of that viewpoint outside the South has caused much of the nation to suppose that such dissatisfaction as existed with the Supreme Court's decision was due to petty prejudice and would soon disappear. That theme has been further developed by the publication of "encouraging" reports of school-integration experiences here and there below the Mason-Dixon Line. Those reports may be true of some Border States and of predominantly white areas in mountain sections of the South; it is not true of any section where Negroes constitute as much as 10 per cent of the population.

The problem is numerical as well as legal, educational, and—in recognition of the Supreme Court's concern—sociological.

The corruption of the Reconstruction era is a matter of recorded history. The memory of the sufferings endured by the white people of the South is an inheritance. It was during this "tragic era" that the Fourteenth Amendment was literally forced upon the helpless States of the South.

When the white people finally wrested control of the State governments from the carpetbaggers and newly freed slaves, and the army of occupation was withdrawn, the South started on the long road to recovery. Agriculture and industry were gradually restored. A public-school system was developed.

No one then seriously asserted that mixing the races in the schools was contemplated by the Fourteenth Amendment. In the constitutions of most of the States of the union, not just those of the South, provisions were adopted for the segregation of the races in the schools.

In 1896 in a case known as *Plessy* v. *Ferguson*, involving a statute providing for segregation of the races on railroad trains, the United States Supreme Court held that a statute providing for separate but equal facilities was not in violation of the Fourteenth Amendment to the Constitution. Thereafter, the Supreme Court in several cases involving schools upheld this doctrine.

Later, the Court, when it included such great judges as Chief Justice Taft and Justices Holmes, Brandeis and Stone, unanimously said that segregation in public schools had been "many times decided to be within the constitutional power of the State legislatures to settle without interference of the federal courts under the Federal Constitution."

Relying upon the stability of the law of the land, and upon the guarantee of State sovereignty in the Federal Constitution, the people of the South invested hundreds of millions of dollars in separate schools for the races. Under this segregated school system, the Southern Negro made greater progress than any other body of Negro people in the history of the world.

The facilities for Negro students in many States were not equal to the facilities provided for white students. The degree of equality differed not only in States, but in counties within a State. The situation in South Carolina was typical of the South. As a rule, the facilities for Negro students in the urban centers were superior to the facilities provided in rural areas. The same was true of facilities for white students. Schools were dependent upon local taxation, and much of the inequality was due to the greater value of industrial property and higher income of the city dweller.

A realization of the inequality that existed between rural schools and urban schools, as well as between the races, influenced me greatly to become a candidate for Governor of South Carolina in 1950.

In my inaugural address I advocated a bond issue of 75 million dollars and the levying of a sales tax of 3 per cent for the purpose of equalizing the school facilities. In presenting this, I said:

"It is our duty to provide for the races substantial equality in school facilities. We should do it because it is right. For me, that is sufficient reason."

Of the 75 million dollars authorized, 70 per cent was allocated to Negro schools even though the Negro-school enrollment constitutes but 39 per cent of the total school enrollment.

Subsequently, the bond issue was increased until it is now 137.5 million dollars. In every school district there is a high school for Negroes and more than one elementary school. On the whole, the Negro school buildings are superior to the white schools because they are modern. The number of Negroes transported by bus to those schools was increased 450 per cent in three years.

Similar educational programs have been under way in other Southern States.

In South Carolina, with a Negro population of 823,622, there are 7,500 Negro schoolteachers, whereas in 12 States east of the Mississippi and north of the Mason-Dixon Line, with a Negro population of 3,351,402, there are only 7,712 Negro teachers. There is no difference in the scale of pay for white and Negro teachers.

About the time the educational program was inaugurated in South Carolina, there was pending in the United States court a case from Clarendon County, asking equal facilities for Negro schools. Later that suit was withdrawn, and a suit was brought by the same complainants, asking the court to declare unconstitutional all segregation laws.

The three-judge court, presided over by Judge Parker, senior judge of the Fourth Circuit, held that under the decisions of the United States Supreme Court from 1896 to that date, the segregation provisions of the Constitution and statutes of South Carolina were not in violation of the Fourteenth Amendment. The lawyers for the National Association for the Advancement of Colored People appealed the case to the United States Supreme Court.

In that Court, the case for Clarendon County was argued by the late Hon. John W. Davis. He was so convinced of the soundness of the decision of the three-judge court that he agreed to argue the case and declined to accept compensation for his services.

Had the Court been unanimous in the view that segregation statutes were in violation of the Fourteenth Amendment, such an opinion would have been written within a few months.

Instead, after many months, the Court announced that the cases should be reargued, and counsel should direct their arguments to certain questions.

The first question was:

"What evidence is there that the Congress which submitted and the State legislatures and conventions which ratified the Fourteenth Amendment, contemplated, or did not contemplate, understood, or did not understand, that it would abolish segregation in public schools?"

Such a question would not have been asked if a majority of the Court was already satisfied that Congress and the State legislatures *did* contemplate that the amendment would prohibit segregation in public schools.

Attorneys representing the parties involved and the attorneys general of many States having segregation statutes filed briefs. The overwhelming preponderance of the legislative history demonstrated that abolishing segregation in schools was not contemplated by the framers of the Fourteenth Amendment, or by the States. . . .

The Court, in its opinion, did not admit . . . the conclusiveness of the evidence that the Fourteenth Amendment did not apply to school segregation. The Court said the evidence was "inconclusive."

Our Constitution is a written instrument. The Fourteenth Amendment does not specifically mention public schools. Having decided unanimously that the legislative history was not "conclusive" that the Congress or the States intended it should apply to schools, one would think the Court would have stopped there and upheld the previous decisions of the Court. Instead, it proceeded to reverse those decisions and legislate a policy for schools. . . .

Frequently, the Court has applied a constitutional principle to subjects not specifically mentioned in the Constitution, and not conceived of by its framers. That has been done, for instance, in applying the "commerce clause" to congressional legislation affecting forms of transportation and communication not in existence when the "commerce clause" was adopted. Material progress, which could not have been anticipated, justified the Court in applying the principle of the "commerce clause" and sustaining the laws affecting commerce between the States.

Ordinarily, the Court has been controlled by legal precedents. In the segregation opinion, it could cite no legal precedent for its decision because all the precedents sustain the doctrine of separate but equal facilities.

In 23 of the States that ratified the Fourteenth Amendment, the courts of last resort held it did not abolish segregation. The Supreme Court itself, in six cases decided over a period of 75 years, upheld the doctrine of equal but separate facilities.

The Court ignored all of these legal precedents and the Constitution and said, "We cannot turn the clock back to 1868 when the amendment was adopted, or even to 1896 when *Plessy* v. *Ferguson* was written."

Why not? The function of the Court is to interpret the Constitution, not amend it. Heretofore, whenever in doubt about the proper interpretation of the Constitution or a statute, the Court has turned the clock back to the time of adoption to ascertain the intent of the draftsmen. When the Court states, "We cannot turn the clock back to 1868," will it ever consider the intent of the framers of the Constitution in 1787?

If the age of a constitutional provision is to be held against its soundness, what about the age of our religion? If time invalidates truth in one field, will it not do so in another?

If the Court could not turn the clock back in these cases, why did it ask counsel for the litigants and the attorneys general of all interested States to file briefs as to the intent of the Congress in 1868, in submitting, and the States, in ratifying, the amendments?

And why were counsel asked to argue whether the Court was bound by its previous decisions, such as *Plessy* v. *Ferguson?*

It is apparent that, when the Court found the legislative history it requested was overwhelming against the conclusion it had reached, it declared the evidence "inconclusive," disregarded the Constitution and—invading the legislative field—declared that segregation would retard the development of Negro children.

That was a terrible indictment of the Negro race. Because—whether a person be black, brown or yellow—whenever the Supreme Court says he cannot develop unless while in school he is permitted to sit by the side of white students, the Court brands that person an inferior human being.

Now mark this well! The Court not only ignored the Constitution and its own decisions, but, is establishing a policy for schools, ignored the record in the case.

In support of its decision, after citing K. B. Clark, who was employed by the National Association for the Advancement of Colored People, it cited the writings of a group of psychologists who had not testified in the trial court. Counsel for the States had no opportunity to rebut the opinions of these psychologists. In such procedure there lies danger for all of us!

And the Court was guilty of what it has frequently condemned. As late as 1952 in the case of *Beauharnais* v. *Illinois* (343 U.S. 250) the Court said:

> "It is not within our competence to confirm or deny claims of social scientists as to the dependence of the individual on the position of his racial or religious group in the community."

Counsel had no opportunity to cross-examine these psychologists as to their qualifications as well as their affiliations. However, in the United States Senate on May 26, 1955, Senator Eastland, chairman of the Senate Judiciary Committee, submitted an amazing record of several of the authorities cited by the Court. He said:

> "Then, too, we find cited by the Court as another modern authority on psychology to override our Constitution, one Theodore Brameld, regarding whom the files of the Committee on Un-American Activities of the United States House of Representatives are replete with citations and information. He is cited as having been a member of no less than 10 organizations declared to be communistic, communistic-front, or Communist dominated."

As to E. Franklin Frazier, another authority cited by the Supreme Court, Senator Eastland said, "The files of the Committee on Un-American Activities of the United States House of Representatives contain 18 citations of Frazier's connections with Communist causes in the United States."

In support of its findings, the Court said, "See generally Myrdal, 'An American Dilemma, 1944.'" I have seen it. On page 13, Professor [Gunnar Karl] Myrdal writes that the Constitution of the United States is "impractical and unsuited to modern conditions" and its adoption was "nearly a plot against the common people."

On page 530, Myrdal states, "In the

South the Negro's person and property are practically subject to the whim of any white person who wishes to take advantage of him or to punish him for any real or fancied wrongdoing or insult."

Millions of people, white and colored, know this is absolutely false. Members of the Supreme Court know it is false. It is an insult to the millions of white Southerners.

Senator Eastland also listed some of those who were associated with Myrdal in writing his book. He stated that the files of the House Committee on Un-American Activities show that many of Myrdal's associates are members of organizations cited as subversive by the Department of Justice under Democratic and Republican Administrations.

I am informed by the Senator that no member of the Senate and no responsible person outside of the Senate has challenged the accuracy of his statements on this subject. Loyal Americans of the North, East, South and West should be outraged that the Supreme Court would reverse the law of the land upon no authority other than some books written by a group of psychologists about whose qualifications we know little and about whose loyalty to the United States there is grave doubt.

And loyal Americans should stop and think when the executive branch of the Federal Government brands as subversive organizations whose membership includes certain psychologists, and the Supreme Court cites those psychologists as authority for invalidating the constitutions of 17 States of the union.

Some advocates of integrated schools shudder to think of anyone's criticizing a decision of the Supreme Court or, certainly, *this* decision of the Court. Well, whenever a member of the Court dissents from the majority opinion, he expresses his views and criticizes—sometimes in vigorous language—the Court's opinion. . . .

The decisions of the Supreme Court must be accepted by the courts of the United States and the States, but not necessarily by the court of public opinion. The people are not the creatures of the Court. The Court is the creature of the people.

One hundred representatives of the people in the United States Congress have issued a "manifesto" criticizing this decision. Such criticism is nothing new. There is precedent for criticism by the people. . . .

The fifth section of the Fourteenth Amendment authorizes Congress to enforce *that* amendment. Congress never legislated to require integrated schools because the Fourteenth Amendment did not embrace schools. On the contrary, Congress specifically appropriated for segregated schools in the District of Columbia. Now that the Supreme Court has amended the Constitution to embrace schools, Congress could legislate on the subject but the Supreme Court knows the representatives of the people will not legislate. Therefore, it calls upon the States of the South to enforce its new policy for schools.

The people of the South are law-abiding. They do not talk or even think of armed resistance. They realize the United States Government has the power to enforce a decision of the Supreme Court. But they believe the decision will close many schools, and think that the Court that ignored the Constitution and rendered the decision should assume the responsibility for its enforcement.

It is unrealistic to expect local school officials to destroy the public schools. With few exceptions, school trustees in the South are white men. They are highly respected in their communities. They serve without compensation. Do you think they will force the children of their neighbors into mixed schools? Many trustees will resign. Negroes will not be selected to succeed them. The schools will be closed. . . .

Suppose the Negroes are admitted: It is agreed that the average Negro child, having had little training at home, does not possess the training of the average white child in the same grade and age group. Shall the white children be held back to help the Negroes progress?

The white parents in the District of Columbia can answer that question. They have had some sad experiences in the last year. As a result, approximately 60 per cent of the students in the public schools of the capital of this nation are Negroes. Many white families have moved to Virginia; many, though they can ill afford it, have placed their children in private schools.

If the Negro students are not able to do the work of the white students, can the races be segregated in the classroom and assigned different class work? Would not the scars inflicted upon the Negro child by such segregation be far deeper than the harm done him by associating with only Negro students in segregated schools?

Should the races be mixed in a school, will a board of trustees composed of white men in a Southern State employ Negro teachers? If not, what will happen to the Negro teachers now employed in the South?

Today, high schools in the South are more social institutions than in the past. There is a cafeteria where all students lunch together. There is a gymnasium where students of both sexes engage in various sports.

Athletic contests, as a rule, are held at night. Students, following the team, travel in school buses. When the races have been accustomed to separation in buses, who can assure there will not be serious consequences?

These are only a few of the problems.

There is a fundamental objection to integration. Southerners fear that the purpose of those who lead the fight for integration in schools is to break down social barriers in childhood and the period of adolescence, and ultimately bring about intermarriage of the races. Some Negro leaders deny this. Others admit this objective. Because the white people of the South are unalterably opposed to such intermarriage, they are unalterably opposed to abolishing segregation in schools.

Disraeli said, "No man will treat with indifference the principle of race. It is the key to history."

Pride of race has been responsible for the grouping of people along ethnic lines throughout the world.

Race preservation is the explanation of the political unrest in South Africa. In the United States, it is not peculiar to the white people of the South. For many years, fear of the Japanese influenced legislation in California.

Today, in 23 of the States, intermarriage of the races is prohibited by law. These laws reflect the fear of mongrelization of the race. To prevent this, the white people of the South are willing to make every sacrifice.

It is useless to argue whether the racial instinct is right or wrong. It exists. It is not confined to any race or to any country. It cannot be eliminated from the minds and hearts of people by the views of psychologists or by the order of a court.

The degree of tension between the races depends upon the percentage of Negro population. In Vermont, where there are few Negroes, there is little tension. But in Detroit, Chicago and Washington, where the Negro population is increasing, tension is increasing. . . .

Frequently, the question is asked: Where do we go from here? Solomon, with all his wisdom, could not give a positive answer. We do know that the approximately 40 million white Southerners will do everything that lawfully can be done to prevent the mixing of the races in the schools.

The hope is for voluntary segregation. As the Negro has progressed educationally and economically, a constantly increasing percentage of them have developed a pride of race. That Negro does not want his children forced into schools where they will not be welcomed. He prefers to have them attend schools for Negroes, taught by Negroes. However, recent events indicate such men will be coerced by the National Association for the Advancement of Colored People and Northern Negroes to demand admission to white schools. Therefore, there is fear for the future.

Plans vary. In some States, the legislature has repealed the statute requiring children to attend schools. When the overwhelming majority of the people of a State are opposed to integrated schools, they could not be expected to enforce laws requiring children to attend mixed schools. . . .

If the Supreme Court shall declare unconstitutional all State statutes having, in its opinion, the effect of continuing segregated schools, then as a last resort many States will discontinue public schools. Some financial assistance would be provided for parents, white and colored, sending children to private schools. Such a plan is proposed in Virginia.

By an overwhelming vote in South Carolina in 1952, there was eliminated from the State Constitution the provision that public schools must be provided for "all children between 6 and 21 years of age." The purpose was to permit the Legislature to be free to discontinue public schools should all other efforts fail.

Should this happen, it will be unfortunate for both races. It would be particularly unfortunate for Negroes because they do not have the financial ability to purchase or to build and equip schools. That fact does not deter the reckless leaders of the National Association for the Advancement of Colored People from jeopardizing the continued existence of Negro schools as well as of white schools.

Should the public schools close, the white people of the South will see that an education equal to that given white children is available to the Negro children who are being used as pawns by the National Association for the Advancement of Colored People in an effort to solve overnight a great social problem.

Integration is now demanded in other fields. In South Carolina, for example, there are recreation parks, supported by public funds and equipped with vacation cabins, lakes and other facilities. For the maximum enjoyment of all, and for the preservation of good order, the parks are operated on a segregated basis—some for whites and some for Negroes.

Recently a suit was brought in a federal court to force the admission of Negroes to a park set aside for white people. The General Assembly, rather than wait for another race-mixing decree, promptly and unanimously ordered the park closed. The suit was dismissed by the court. For the future, money is appropriated only for segregated parks. Similar suits have been brought in other States. All parks may soon be closed as a result of litigation inspired by the National Association for the Advancement of Colored People and some Northern sentimentalists who do great injury to their fellow man. Woodrow Wilson once said:

"It will be a bad day for society when sentimentalists are encouraged to suggest all the measures that shall be taken for the betterment of the race."

Tragic as may be the consequences in destroying the public-school system in the South, more frightening are the consequences of the trend of the present Court to destroy the powers of the 48 States.

In the case of *Pennsylvania* v. *Steve Nelson,* decided April 2, 1956, the same Court that declared unconstitutional the segregation statutes of 17 States invalidated the laws of 42 States prohibiting the knowing advocacy of the overthrow of the Government of the United States by violence, as long as there is a federal law against sedition.

The Department of Justice protested to the Court that the State laws did not interfere with the enforcement of the federal statute. But the Court struck down the laws of 42 States. Justices Reed, Burton and Minton vigorously dissented.

One week later the Court declared unconstitutional a provision of the Charter of New York City under which Professor Slochower, an employee, was dismissed for failure to answer a question in an authorized inquiry, on the ground that his answer might incriminate him. It is encouraging to the people that the same three Justices dissented and were joined by Justice Harlan.

Power intoxicates men. It is never voluntarily surrendered. It must be taken from them. The Supreme Court must be curbed.

The Constitution authorizes the Congress to regulate the appellate jurisdiction of the Supreme Court. Loyal Americans who believe in constitutional government appeal to the court of public opinion in the hope that you will urge the Congress to act before it is too late.

The present trend brings joy to Communists and their fellow travelers who want to see all power centered in the Federal Government because they can more easily influence one Government in Washington than the 48 governments in 48 States.

But the trend of the Court is disturbing to millions of Americans who respect the Constitution and believe that in order to preserve the republic we must preserve what is left of the powers of the States.

You may be unconcerned today. You may "Cry Tomorrow."

An outstanding expert on federal procedure and constitutional law, HERBERT WECHSLER (b. 1909) is Harlan Fiske Stone Professor of Constitutional Law at Columbia University, where he has been since 1945. The excerpts below are from his widely noticed and controversial Oliver Wendell Holmes Lecture, delivered at the Harvard Law School in April of 1959. Wechsler criticized some of the important recent opinions of the Supreme Court for failing to abide by what he termed "neutral principles" of constitutional adjudication. The lecture was later printed in the *Harvard Law Review* and then incorporated in a book of essays. In the selection below, Wechsler clearly approves the results of *Brown*, but questions the reasoning of the opinion. Like Cahn, Cook and Potter, he doubts the validity of the social science testimony. But unlike Cahn, he sees no solid alternative ground taken by the Court. What does Wechsler mean when he asserts that the real issue to him is not discrimination but association?*

Herbert Wechsler

The Court Ignored Neutral Principles

. . . I put it to you that the main constituent of the judicial process is precisely that it must be genuinely principled, resting with respect to every step that is involved in reaching judgment on analysis and reasons quite transcending the immediate result that is achieved. To be sure, the courts decide, or should decide, only the case they have before them. But must they not decide on grounds of adequate neutrality and generality, tested not only by the instant application but by others that the principles imply? Is it not the very essence of judicial method to insist upon attending to such other cases, preferably those involving an opposing interest, in evaluating any principle avowed? . . .

Let me repeat what I have thus far tried to say. The courts have both the title and the duty when a case is properly before them to review the actions of the other branches in the light of constitutional provisions, even though the action involves value choices, as invariably action does. In doing so, however, they are bound to function otherwise than as a naked power organ; they participate as courts of law. This calls for facing how determinations of this kind can be

*Reprinted by permission of the publishers from pp. 21, 27, 43–47 of Herbert Wechsler, *Principles, Politics and Fundamental Law* (Cambridge, Mass.: Harvard University Press). Copyright 1961, by the President and Fellows of Harvard College. Footnotes omitted.

asserted to have any legal quality. The answer, I suggest, inheres primarily in that they are—or are obliged to be—entirely principled. A principled decision, in the sense I have in mind, is one that rests on reasons with respect to all the issues in the case, reasons that in their generality and their neutrality transcend any immediate result that is involved. When no sufficient reasons of this kind can be assigned for overturning value choices of the other branches of the Government or of a state, those choices must, of course, survive. Otherwise, as Holmes said in his first opinion for the Court, "a constitution, instead of embodying only relatively fundamental rules of right, as generally understood by all English-speaking communities, would become the partisan of a particular set of ethical or economical opinions. . . ."

The virtue or demerit of a judgment turns, therefore, entirely on the reasons that support it and their adequacy to maintain any choice of values it decrees, or, it is vital that we add, to maintain the rejection of a claim that any given choice should be decreed. . . .

Lastly, I come to the school decision, which for one of my persuasion stirs the deepest conflict I experience in testing the thesis I propose. Yet I would surely be engaged in playing Hamlet without Hamlet if I did not try to state the problems that appear to me to be involved.

The problem for me, I hardly need to say, is not that the Court departed from its earlier decisions holding or implying that the equality of public educational facilities demanded by the Constitution could be met by separate schools. I stand with the long tradition of the Court that previous decisions must be subject to reexamination when a case against their reasoning is made. Nor is the problem that the Court disturbed the settled patterns of a portion of the country; even that must be accepted as a lesser evil than nullification of the Constitution. Nor is it that history does not confirm that an agreed purpose of the fourteenth amendment was to forbid separate schools or that there is important evidence that many thought the contrary; the words are general and leave room for expanding content as time passes and conditions change. Nor is it that the Court may have miscalculated the extent to which its judgment would be honored or accepted; it is not a prophet of the strength of our national commitment to respect the judgments of the courts. Nor is it even that the Court did not remit the issue to the Congress, acting under the enforcement clause of the amendment. That was a possible solution, to be sure, but certainly Professor Freund is right that it would merely have evaded the claims made.

The problem inheres strictly in the reasoning of the opinion, an opinion which is often read with less fidelity by those who praise it than by those by whom it is condemned. The Court did not declare, as many wish it had, that the fourteenth amendment forbids all racial lines in legislation, though subsequent *per curiam* decisions may . . . go that far. Rather, as Judge Hand observed, the separate-but-equal formula was not overruled "in form" but was held to have "no place" in public education on the ground that segregated schools are "inherently unequal," with deleterious effects upon the colored children in implying their inferiority, effects which retard their educational and mental development. So, indeed, the district court had found as a fact in the Kansas case, a finding which the Supreme Court embraced, citing some further "modern authority" in its support.

modest decision actually — it could

Does the validity of the decision turn then on the sufficiency of evidence or of judicial notice to sustain a finding that the separation harms the Negro children who may be involved? There were, indeed, some witnesses who expressed that opinion in the Kansas case, as there were also witnesses in the companion Virginia case . . . whose view[s] . . . [were] to the contrary. Much depended on the question that the witness had in mind, which rarely was explicit. Was he comparing the position of the Negro child in a segregated school with his position in an integrated school where he was happily accepted and regarded by the whites; or was he comparing his position under separation with that under integration where the whites were hostile to his presence and found ways to make their feelings known? And if the harm that segregation worked was relevant, what of the benefits that it entailed: sense of security, the absence of hostility? Were they irrelevant? Moreover, was the finding in Topeka applicable without more to Clarendon County, South Carolina, with 2799 colored students and only 295 whites? Suppose that more Negroes in a community preferred separation than opposed it? Would that be relevant to whether they were hurt or aided by segregation as opposed to integration? Their fates would be governed by the change of system quite as fully as those of the students who complained.

I find it hard to think the judgment really turned upon the facts. Rather, it seems to me, it must have rested on the view that racial segregation is, in principle, a denial of equality to the minority against whom it is directed; that is, the group that is not dominant politically and, therefore, does not make the choice involved. For many who support the Court's decision this assuredly is the decisive ground. But this position also presents problems. Does it not involve an inquiry into the motive of the legislature, which is generally foreclosed to the courts? Is it alternatively defensible to make the measure of validity of legislation the way it is interpreted by those who are affected by it? In the context of a charge that segregation *with equal facilities* is a denial of equality, is there not a point in *Plessy* in the statement that if "enforced separation stamps the colored race with a badge of inferiority" it is solely because its members choose "to put that construction upon it"? Does enforced separation of the sexes discriminate against females merely because it may be the females who resent it and it is imposed by judgments predominantly male? Is a prohibition of miscegenation a discrimination against the colored member of the couple who would like to marry?

For me, assuming equal facilities, the question posed by state-enforced segregation is not one of discrimination at all. Its human and its constitutional dimensions lie entirely elsewhere, in the denial by the state of freedom to associate, a denial that impinges in the same way on any groups or races that may be involved. I think, and I hope not without foundation, that the Southern white also pays heavily for segregation, not only in the sense of guilt that he must carry but also in the benefits he is denied. In the days when I was joined with Charles H. Houston in a litigation in the Supreme Court, before the present building was constructed, he did not suffer more than I in knowing that we had to go to Union Station to lunch together during the recess. Does not the problem of miscegenation show most clearly that it is the freedom of association that at bottom is involved, the only case, I may add, where it is implicit in the situation that association is desired by the only individuals involved? . . .

But if the freedom of association is denied by segregation, integration forces an association upon those for whom it is unpleasant or repugnant. Is this not the heart of the issue involved, a conflict in human claims of high dimension, not unlike many others that involve the highest freedoms. . . . Given a situation where the state must practically choose between denying the association to those individuals who wish it or imposing it on those who would avoid it, is there a basis in neutral principles for holding that the Constitution demands that the claims for association should prevail? I should like to think there is, but I confess that I have not yet written the opinion. To write it is for me the challenge of the school-segregation cases.

Currently Henry R. Luce Professor of Jurisprudence at Yale Law School, CHARLES L. BLACK, JR. (b. 1915) has been a strong and consistent spokesman for the view, most associated with Justice William O. Douglas, that maintains that the Supreme Court should take an active, positive role in behalf of civil liberties and equal rights. Black's 1961 book, *The People and the Court,* makes a persuasive case for the democratic legitimacy of judicial review. Reared in Texas in a southern-oriented town, Black combines personal experience with professional skill in this analysis of the "lawfulness" of the segregation decisions. How does Black's discussion of the association issue compare with Wechsler's, who raised the matter in his lecture? How does Black's view of the Court's *opinion* compare with Edmond Cahn's?*

Charles L. Black, Jr.

The Court Upheld the Constitution

If the cases outlawing segregation were wrongly decided, then they ought to be overruled. One can go further: if dominant professional opinion ever forms and settles on the belief that they were wrongly decided, then they will be overruled, slowly or all at once, openly or silently. The insignificant error, however palpable, can stand, because the convenience of settlement outweighs the discomfort of error. But the hugely consequential error cannot stand and does not stand.

There is pragmatic meaning then, there is call for action, in the suggestion that the segregation cases cannot be justified.[1] In the long run, as a corollary, there is practical and not merely intellectual significance in the question whether these cases were rightly decided. I think they were rightly decided, by overwhelming weight of reason, and I intend here to say why I hold this belief.

My liminal difficulty is rhetorical—or, perhaps more accurately, one of fashion. Simplicity is out of fashion, and the basic scheme of reasoning on which these cases can be justified is awkwardly simple. First, the equal protection clause of the

[1] See Wechsler, *Toward Neutral Principles of Constitutional Law,* 73 Harv. L. Rev. 1, 34 (1959).

The present Article was immediately suggested by Professor Wechsler's questionings. It is not, however, to be looked on as formal "reply," since I cover here only one part of the ground he goes over, and since my lines of thought are only partly responsive in terms to the questions as he sees them.

* Charles L. Black, Jr., "The Lawfulness of the Segregation Decisions." Reprinted by permission of the Yale Law Journal Company and Fred B. Rothman & Company from *The Yale Law Journal,* Vol. 69. pp. 421-430 (January 1960). Most footnotes omitted.

fourteenth amendment should be read as saying that the Negro race, as such, is not to be significantly disadvantaged by the laws of the states. Secondly, segregation is a massive intentional disadvantaging of the Negro race, as such, by state law. No subtlety at all. Yet I cannot disabuse myself of the idea that that is really all there is to the segregation cases. If both these propositions can be supported by the preponderance of argument, the cases were rightly decided. If they cannot be so supported, the cases are in perilous condition.

As a general thing, the first of these propositions has so far as I know never been controverted in a holding of the Supreme Court. . . . If *Plessy* v. *Ferguson* be thought a faltering from this principle, I step back to the principle itself. But the *Plessy* Court clearly conceived it to be its task to show that segregation did not really disadvantage the Negro, except through his own choice. . . .[2] the fault of *Plessy* is in the psychology and sociology of its minor premise. . . .

What the fourteenth amendment, in its historical setting, must be read to say is that the Negro is to enjoy equal protection of the laws, and that the fact of his being a Negro is not to be taken to be a good enough reason for denying him this equality, however "reasonable" that might seem to some people. All possible arguments, however convincing, for discriminating against the Negro, were finally rejected by the fourteenth amendment.

It is sometimes urged that a special qualification was written on the concept of "equality" by the history of the adoption of the amendment—that an intent can be made out to exclude segregation from those legal discriminations invalidated by the requirement of equality, whether or not it actually works inequality. . . . The question of the "intent" of the men of 1866 on segregation *as we know it* calls for a far chancier guess than is commonly supposed, for they were unacquainted with the institution as it prevails in the American South today. To guess their verdict upon the institution as it functions in the midtwentieth century supposes an imaginary hypothesis which grows more preposterous as it is sought to be made more vivid. They can in the nature of the case have bequeathed us only their generalities; the specifics lay unborn as they disbanded. . . .

Then does segregation offend against equality? Equality, like all general concepts, has marginal areas where philosophic difficulties are encountered. But if a whole race of people finds itself confined within a system which is set up and continued for the very purpose of keeping it in an inferior station, and if the question is then solemnly propounded whether such a race is being treated "equally," I think we ought to exercise one of the sovereign prerogatives of philosophers—that of laughter. The only question remaining (after we get our laughter under control) is whether the segregation system answers to this description.

Here I must confess to a tendency to start laughing all over again. I was raised in the South, in a Texas city where the pattern of segregation was firmly fixed. I am sure it never occurred to anyone, white or colored, to question its meaning. The fiction of "equality" is just about on

[2] "We consider the underlying fallacy of the plaintiff's argument to consist in the assumption that the enforced separation of the two races stamps the colored race with a badge of inferiority. *If this be so, it is not by reason of anything found in the act, but solely because the colored race chooses to put that construction upon it.*" (Emphasis added.) The curves of callousness and stupidity intersect at their respective maxima.

a level with the fiction of "finding" in the action of trover. I think few candid southerners deny this. Northern people may be misled by the entirely sincere protestations of many southerners that segregation is "better" for the Negroes, is not intended to hurt them. But I think a little probing would demonstrate that what is meant is that it is better for the Negroes to accept a position of inferiority, at least for the indefinite future.

But the subjectively obvious, if queried, must be backed up by more public materials. What public materials assure me that my reading of the social meaning of segregation is not a mere idiosyncracy?

First, of course, is history. Segregation in the South comes down in apostolic succession from slavery and the *Dred Scott* case. The South fought to keep slavery, and lost. Then it tried the Black Codes, and lost. Then it looked around for something else and found segregation. The movement for segregation was an integral part of the movement to maintain and further "white supremacy"; its triumph (as Professor Woodward has shown) represented a triumph of extreme racialist over moderate sentiment about the Negro. It is now defended very largely on the ground that the Negro as such is not fit to associate with the white.

History, too, tells us that segregation was imposed on one race by the other race; consent was not invited or required. Segregation in the South grew up and is kept going because and only because the white race has wanted it that way—an incontrovertible fact which in itself hardly consorts with equality. This fact perhaps more than any other confirms the picture which a casual or deep observer is likely to form of the life of a southern community—a picture not of mutual separation of whites and Negroes, but of one in-group enjoying full normal communal life and one out-group that is barred from this life and forced into an inferior life of its own. . . .

Segregation is historically and contemporaneously associated in a functioning complex with practices which are indisputably and grossly discriminatory. I have in mind especially the long-continued and still largely effective exclusion of Negroes from voting. Here we have two things. First, a certain group of people is "segregated." Secondly, at about the same time, the very same group of people, down to the last man and woman, is barred, or sought to be barred, from the common political life of the community—from all political power. Then we are solemnly told that segregation is not intended to harm the segregated race, or to stamp it with the mark of inferiority. How long must we keep a straight face?

Here it may be added that, generally speaking, segregation is the pattern of law in communities where the extralegal patterns of discrimination against Negroes are the tightest, where Negroes are subjected to the strictest codes of "unwritten law" as to job opportunities, social intercourse, patterns of housing, going to the back door, being called by the first name, saying "Sir," and all the rest of the whole sorry business. . . .

The various items I have mentioned differ in weight; not every one would suffice in itself to establish the character of segregation. Taken together they are of irrefragable strength. The society that has just lost the Negro as a slave, that has just lost out in an attempt to put him under quasi-servile "Codes," the society that views his blood as a contamination and his name as an insult, the society that extralegally imposes on him every humiliating mark of low caste and that until yesterday kept him in line by lynching—this society, careless of his consent, moves by law, first to exclude him from voting, and secondly to cut him off from mixing in the general public life of the community. The Court that refused to see inequality in this cutting off would be making the only kind of law that can be warranted outrageous in advance—a law based on self-induced blindness, on flagrant contradiction of known fact.

I have stated all these points shortly because they are matters of common notoriety, matters not so much for judicial notice as for the background knowledge of educated men who live in the world. A court may advise itself of them as it advises itself of the facts that we are a "religious people," that the country is more industrialized than in Jefferson's day, that children are the natural objects of fathers' bounty, that criminal sanctions are commonly thought to deter, that steel is a basic commodity in our economy, that the imputation of unchastity is harmful to a woman. Such judgments, made on such a basis, are in the foundations of all law, decisional as well as statutory; it would be the most unneutral of principles, improvised *ad hoc,* to require that a court faced with the present problem refuse to note a plain fact about the society of the United States—the fact that the social meaning of segregation is the putting of the Negro in a position of walled-off inferiority—or the other equally plain fact that such treatment is hurtful to human beings. Southern courts, on the basis of just such a judgment, have held that the placing of a white person in a Negro railroad car is an actionable humiliation; must a court pretend not to know that the Negro's situation there is humiliating?

I think that some of the artificial mist of puzzlement called into being around this question originates in a single fundamental mistake. The issue is seen in terms of what might be called the metaphysics of sociology: "Must Segregation Amount to Discrimination?" That is an interesting question; someday the methods of sociology may be adequate to answering it. But it is not our question. Our question is whether discrimination inheres in that segregation which is imposed by law in the twentieth century in certain specific states in the American Union. And that question has meaning and can find an answer only on the ground of history and of common knowledge about the facts of life in the times and places aforesaid.

Now I need not and do not maintain that the evidence is all one way; it never is on issues of burning, fighting concern. Let us not question here the good faith of those who assert that segregation represents no more than an attempt to furnish a wholesome opportunity for parallel development of the races; let us rejoice at the few scattered instances they can bring forward to support their view of the matter. But let us then ask which balance-pan flies upward.

The case seems so onesided that it is hard to make out what is being protested against when it is asked, rhetorically, how the Court can possibly advise itself of the real character of the segregation system. It seems that what is being said is that, while no actual doubt exists as to what segregation is for and what kind of societal pattern it supports and implements, there is no ritually sanctioned way in which the Court, as a Court, can permissibly learn what is obvious to everybody else and to the Justices as individuals. But surely, confronted with such a problem, legal acumen has only one proper task—that of developing ways to make it permissible for the Court to use what it knows; any other counsel is of despair. And, equally surely, the fact that the Court has assumed as true a matter of common knowledge in regard to broad societal patterns, is (to say the very least) pretty far down the list of things to protest against.

I conclude, then, that the Court had the soundest reasons for judging that segregation violates the fourteenth amendment. These reasons make up the simple syllogism with which I began: The fourteenth amendment commands equality, and segregation as we know it is inequality.

Let me take up a few peripheral points. It is true that the specifically hurtful character of segregation, as a net matter in the life of each segregated individual, may be hard to establish. It seems enough to say of this . . . that no such demand is made as to other constitutional rights. To have a confession beaten out of one might in some particular case be the beginning of a new and better life. To be subjected to a racially differentiated curfew might be the best thing in the world for some individual boy. A man might ten years later go back to thank the policeman who made him get off the platform and stop making a fool of himself. Religious persecution proverbially strengthens faith. We do not ordinarily go that far, or look so narrowly into the matter. That a practice, on massive historical evidence and in common sense, has the designed and generally apprehended effect of putting its victims at a disadvantage, is enough for law. At least it always has been enough.

I can heartily concur in the judgment that segregation harms the white as much as it does the Negro. Sadism rots the policeman; the suppressor of thought loses light; the community that forms into a mob, and goes down and dominates a trial, may wound itself beyond healing. Can this reciprocity of hurt, this fated mutuality that inheres in all inflicted wrong, serve to validate the wrong itself?

Finally it is doubtless true that the *School Segregation Cases,* and perhaps others of the cases on segregation, represented a choice between two kinds of freedom of association. Freedom from the massive wrong of segregation entails a corresponding loss of freedom on the part of the whites who must now associate with Negroes on public occasions, as we all must on such occasions associate with many persons we had rather not associate with. It is possible to state the competing claims in symmetry, and to ask whether there are constitutional reasons for preferring the Negroes' desire for merged participation in public life to the white man's desire to live a public life without Negroes in proximity.

The question must be answered, but I would approach it in a way which seems to me more normal—the way in which we more usually approach comparable symmetries that might be stated as to all other asserted rights. The fourteenth amendment forbids inequality, forbids the disadvantaging of the Negro race by law. It was surely anticipated that the following of this directive would entail some disagreeableness for some white southerners. The disagreeableness might take many forms; the white man, for example, might dislike having a Negro neighbor in the exercise of the latter's equal right to own a home, or dislike serving on a jury with a Negro, or dislike having Negroes on the streets with him after ten o'clock. When the directive of equality cannot be followed without displeasing the white, then something that can be called a "freedom" of the white must be impaired. If the fourteenth amendment commands equality, and if segregation violates equality, then the status of the reciprocal "freedom" is automatically settled.

I find reinforcement here, at least as a matter of spirit, in the fourteenth amendment command that Negroes shall be "citizens" of their States. It is hard for me to imagine in what operative sense a man could be a "citizen" without his fellow citizens' once in a while having to associate with him. If, for example, his "citizenship" results in his election to the School Board, the white members may (as recently in Houston) put him off to one side of the room, but there is still some impairment of their freedom "not to associate." That freedom, in fact, exists only at home; in public, we have to associate with anybody who has a right to be there. The question of our right not to associate with him is concluded when we decide whether he has a right to be there. . . .

These judgments, like all judgments, must rest on the rightness of their law and the truth of their fact. Their law is right if the equal protection clause in the fourteenth amendment is to be taken as stating, without arbitrary exceptions, a broad principle of practical equality for the Negro race, inconsistent with any device that in fact relegates the Negro race to a position of inferiority. Their facts are true if it is true that the segregation system is actually conceived and does actually function as a means of keeping the Negro in a status of inferiority. I dare say at this time that in the end the decisions will be accepted by the profession on just that basis. Opinions composed under painful stresses may leave much to be desired.[3] . . . But the judgments, in law and in fact, are as right and true as any that ever was uttered.

[3] I do not mean here to join the hue and cry against the *Brown* opinion. The charge that it is "sociological" is either a truism or a canard—a truism if it means that the Court, precisely like the *Plessy* Court, and like innumerable other courts facing innumerable other issues of law, had to resolve and did resolve a question about social fact; a canard if it means that anything like principal reliance was placed on the formally "scientific" authorities, which are relegated to a footnote and treated as merely corroboratory of common sense. It seems to me that the venial fault of the opinion consists in its not spelling out that segregation, for reasons of the kind I have brought forward in this Article, is perceptibly a means of ghettoizing the imputedly inferior race. . . . That such treatment is generally not good for children needs less talk than the Court gives it.

Former law librarian and now professor of law at Rutgers University School of Law, ALBERT P. BLAUSTEIN (b. 1921) is also a coauthor with Robert L. Zangrando of a 670-page documentary on *Civil Rights and the American Negro* (1968). CLARENCE CLYDE FERGUSON, Jr. (b. 1924), dean and professor of law at Howard University, was former General Counsel for the United States Commission on Civil Rights. Their popular work *Desegregation and the Law* (1957) was the first full-scale attempt to examine the historical background, legal development, and future implications of the *Brown* decision. The excerpt below traces the dramatic impact of the *Brown* case on other areas of segregation besides public schools. Why did the Supreme Court never explicitly overrule the *Plessy* decision by name, although accomplishing the same thing by other means?*

Albert P. Blaustein
Clarence Clyde Ferguson, Jr.

The Judicial Destruction of "Separate but Equal"

Brown v. *Board of Education* was not long confined to the legal pigeonhole labeled "school segregation." Overriding the contentions of Southern counsel, the various courts—including the Supreme Court—have refused to limit the mandates of May 17, 1954, and May 31, 1955, to specific holdings and specific facts. Within two years after "Black Monday," a score and more of judicial decisions had recorded the wide swath which the Brown case had cut in other areas of racial segregation: in transportation, housing, parks and recreational facilities. The reasoning of *Brown* v. *Board of Education* had signaled the end of racial discrimination by law in the United States.

Some of this was inevitable. Education is not restricted to the classroom. Public school integration automatically calls for the desegregation of extracurricular activities connected with the learning process. It also calls for an end to the separation of whites and Negroes on their way to and from, as well as within, the schoolhouse. Desegregated schoolrooms represent but lip-service compliance while school buses remain segregated—and especially when limited transportation may be kept limited as a practical means of thwarting integration decrees. . . .

*Albert P. Blaustein and Clarence Clyde Ferguson, Jr., *Desegregation and the Law, The Meaning and Effect of the School Segregation Cases* (New Brunswick, N.J.: Rutgers University Press, 1957). Reprinted by permission of Rutgers University Press. Footnotes omitted.

Exactly one week after "Black Monday," the Supreme Court rendered three *per curiam* decisions extending the effect of *Brown* v. *Board of Education* beyond the borders of public school segregation. Two of those cases were in the field of higher education; the third was concerned with the use of golf courses, swimming pools, athletic facilities and an amphitheater in the city parks of Louisville, Kentucky. All three of those decisions were duly recorded on the same page of the official *United States Reports.* All three contained the identical forty words and six numbers. All three remanded the controversies in issue to the lower courts "for consideration in the light of the Segregation Cases decided May 17, 1954 . . . and conditions that now prevail."

While no subsequent decision was rendered in the Kentucky parks case, the omission is not significant. Other courts and other cases have opened public parks, public golf courses and public beaches to members of the colored race, all on the authority of the school segregation opinions. It has happened in Georgia, Texas and Virginia, as well as in Maryland, Tennessee and, of course, Kentucky.

The landmark case in this area is the bathing-beach dispute of *Mayor and City Council of Baltimore City* v. *Dawson,* affirmed by the Supreme Court on November 7, 1955. The action, based on the "separate but equal" doctrine of *Plessy* v. *Ferguson* and two lower court decisions dealing directly with public recreation, had originally been dismissed in the federal district court. . . .

Plaintiffs appealed—and here is what the Fourth Circuit Court (comprising the states of Maryland, North Carolina, South Carolina, Virginia and West Virginia) said on March 14, 1955: "Our view is that the authority of these cases was swept away by the subsequent decisions of the Supreme Court. . . . It is now obvious . . . that segregation cannot be justified as a means to preserve the public peace merely because the tangible facilities furnished to one race are equal to those furnished to the other. The Supreme Court expressed the opinion in *Brown* v. *Board of Education* . . . that it must consider public education in the light of its full development and its present place in American life, and . . . must also take into account the psychological factors recognized at this time, including the feeling of inferiority generated in the hearts and minds of Negro children, when separated solely because of their race from those of similar age and qualification." Then came the even more significant statement:

"With this in mind, it is obvious that racial segregation in recreational activities can no longer be sustained as a proper exercise of the police power of the State, for if that power cannot be invoked to sustain racial segregation in the schools, where attendance is compulsory and racial friction may be apprehended from the enforced comingling of the races, it cannot be sustained with respect to public beach and bathhouse facilities, the use of which is entirely optional."

Squarely before the Supreme Court were two widely divergent interpretations of the meaning of *Brown* v. *Board of Education.* By reversing the court of appeals (thus agreeing with the district court) the nine men would have been making a distinction between school segregation and other types of racial classification. They would have been saying, in effect, that school segregation statutes are unconstitutional only because they are "unreasonable"—or that school segregation is invalid *per se,* but that segregation by race might be constitutionally justified in fields other than education.

But the Supreme Court did not reverse

Judge Parker's court. On November 7, 1955, the nine men specifically affirmed the decision of the court of appeals and the interpretation of *Brown* v. *Board of Education* contained in that decision. All racial classification had been held unconstitutional *per se*.

Within a year, four similar decisions were handed down in Virginia, Texas, Kentucky and Tennessee. . . .

Citing the Dawson case, together with a Florida decision which is not important to this discussion and the action of the Supreme Court in remanding the Louisville, Kentucky, parks dispute, a Texas federal court had this to say: "It is true that the School Segregation Cases expressly overrule *Plessy* v. *Ferguson* only insofar as it applied to the field of public education, but it seems clear to me that [these other decisions] are strong indications that *Plessy* v. *Ferguson* will not, and should not, be held to be controlling in the public recreational field. If the provisions for equal tangible facilities in the field of public education do not eliminate intangible or psychological discrimination in the field of public education, how can it reasonably be said the equality in tangibles in the field of public recreation eliminates psychological factors so clearly involved in segregation based upon the color of a man's skin? It can, of course, be argued that the intangibles are less effective in the public recreational field than in the field of public education, but that is to say that a little discrimination is to be condoned, but a great deal should be condemned. If the reasoning in the School Segregation Cases concerning psychological factors is sound as it relates to public education, then it must necessarily apply to the field of public recreation." . . .

These cases represented comparatively easy victories for the desegregation forces. Not so the Georgia dispute of *Holmes* v. *City of Atlanta*. Four decisions were handed down in the course of litigation. On July 8, 1954, the federal district court found that municipal golf courses had not been furnished for the colored, and ordered the city to permit Negroes to share existing facilities on a "substantially equal basis." Segregation was to be permitted. In the Brown case, according to the court, "the doctrine of 'separate but equal' was rejected only as it applied to public education." The decision was affirmed by the United States Court of Appeals for the Fifth Circuit nearly a year later, on June 17, 1955. The Supreme Court said "no." On November 7, 1955, the nine men vacated the judgments below and ordered the district court to enter a decree in conformity with the Dawson decision. Compliance was effected on December 22, 1955, when the lower court enjoined "any distinction on account of race or color" on the Atlanta golf courses and "further ordered that this judgment and decree take effect immediately." . . .

Save for the lower court decisions in Georgia, the judicial opinions since May 17, 1954, have reflected a clear, steady trend toward total desegregation. Yet there was some technical legal support for the Georgia position. *Brown* v. *Board of Education* was a case involving school segregation, and school segregation only. It did not overrule *Plessy* v. *Ferguson*. It could not. *Plessy* v. *Ferguson* was a case involving public transportation, not public schools. The nine men said only that "separate but equal" as set forth in *Plessy* v. *Ferguson* "has no place" in public education.

Discounted, discredited or studiously avoided in every discrimination controversy which came before the Supreme Court in the two and one-half years following *Brown* v. *Board of Education*, the case of *Plessy* v. *Ferguson* still remained a barrier in the path of total desegregation. Southern lawyers—and a few Southern judges—refused to recognize the fact that *Brown* v. *Board of Education* had declared all racial classifications unconstitutional *per se*, and attempted to limit the impact of that decision to cases involving the public schools.

Since only in a transportation case could the nine men overrule the "separate but equal" doctrine of *Plessy* v. *Ferguson*, the legal profession watched with interest as bus cases from South Carolina and Alabama began the course of trial and appeal which would lead to Supreme Court decision.

The cases were *Flemming* v. *South Carolina Electric and Gas Company* and the famous Montgomery, Alabama, case of *Gayle* v. *Browder*.

The Flemming dispute was the first to reach the courts. A Negro woman sued a bus company for damages because a bus driver made her change her seat in accordance with South Carolina's segregation laws. Federal District Court Judge George Bell Timmerman, Sr., dismissed the action, contending that the state statutes complained of were valid under *Plessy* v. *Ferguson*. The appeal arrived for decision before the Fourth Circuit Court of Appeals on July 14, 1955. A *per curiam* opinion was rendered, reversing the lower court action and remanding the case for further proceedings in accordance with the judgment of the appellate tribunal. Judge John J. Parker presided. Wrote the court: "We do not think that the separate but equal doctrine of *Plessy* v. *Ferguson* . . . can any longer be regarded as a correct statement of the law. That case recognizes segregation of the races by common carriers as being governed by the same principles as segregation in the public schools, and the recent decisions in *Brown* v. *Board of Education* . . . which relate to public schools, leave no doubt that the separate but equal doctrine approved in *Plessy* v. *Ferguson* has been repudiated. That the principle applied in the school cases should be applied in cases involving transportation, appears quite clearly. . . ."

This decision was immediately appealed to the United States Supreme Court. In April, 1956, however, the Supreme Court ruled that the appeal had been prematurely brought, and refused to hear the case until it had been reconsidered in Judge Timmerman's court.

Six weeks later, while the Flemming case was still before Judge Timmerman, came the first opinion in *Gayle* v. *Browder*. A special three-judge district court heard the case and concluded—with one judge dissenting—that Judge Parker's court was right. "We cannot in good conscience," wrote the majority, "perform our duty as judges by blindly following the precedent of *Plessy* v. *Ferguson* . . . when our study leaves us in complete agreement with the fourth circuit's opinion in *Flemming* v. *South Carolina Electric and Gas Company* . . . that the separate but equal doctrine can no longer be safely followed as a correct statement of the law. In fact, we think that *Plessy* v. *Ferguson* has been impliedly though not explicitly overruled, and that, under the later decision, there is now no rational basis upon which the separate but equal doctrine can be validly applied to public carrier transportation within the City of Montgomery." . . .

Gayle v. *Browder* came before the Supreme Court for final decision on November 13, 1956. As was to be expected, the nine men unanimously affirmed the opinion below—the opinion which declared invalid the state statutes which had required racial segregation on the buses of Montgomery, Alabama. As was to be expected, they based their determination on the precedents of *Brown* v. *Board of Education,* the bathing-beach dispute of *Mayor and City Council of Baltimore City* v. *Dawson* and the Georgia golf course case of *Holmes* v. *Atlanta.*

The New York *Times* characterized the decision as having "placed a headstone at the grave of Plessy v. Ferguson." And this despite the fact that the Supreme Court had studiously avoided mentioning the 1896 determination by name. No opinion was written in *Gayle* v. *Browder.* The decision was rendered *per curiam* merely noting the affirmance. Yet the case must stand as a specific restatement of the *per se* meaning of *Brown* v. *Board of Education* and as a specific rejection of the Plessy concept in the transportation field. *Plessy* v. *Ferguson* may not have been overruled by name, but it was overruled all the same. The "separate but equal" doctrine has finally become a constitutional nullity.

LOREN MILLER (1903–1967), the son of a former slave, was a judge of the Municipal Court of Los Angeles at the time of his death. A former vice-president of the NAACP, member of the National Committee of the American Civil Liberties Union, and a leader of the National Bar Association (an organization of black lawyers), Miller dedicated his life to the pursuit of equal justice under law for all people. His book *The Petitioners* (1966) is the most detailed study of the history of the Supreme Court and the Negro. Although critical of many of the Court's decisions, he retained a strong faith in the ultimate justness of the legal and constitutional processes. In this selection he describes the manifold devices used by southern obstructionists to avoid implementation of the Court's decision in *Brown*. The Court's enforcement formula of "all deliberate speed," he holds, played into the hands of southern resistance.*

Loren Miller

"All Deliberate Speed" a Mistake

. . . Chief Justice Warren again spoke for a unanimous Court on May 31, 1955. He explained that "Full implementation of . . . constitutional principles may require solution of varied local school problems. School authorities have the primary responsibility for . . . solving these problems; courts will have to consider whether the action of school authorities constitutes good faith implementation of the governing constitutional principles. Because of their proximity to local conditions and the possible need for further hearings, the courts which originally heard these cases can best perform this judicial appraisal. Accordingly, we believe it appropriate to remand the cases to those courts."

The courts to which the cases were remanded were admonished to apply equitable principles that would be fair to both the Negro children and school authorities but, he said, "it should go without saying that the vitality of these constitutional principles cannot be allowed to yield simply because of disagreement with them." The courts were also told to "require that the defendants make a prompt and reasonable start toward full compliance with our May 17, 1954, decision. . . . Once such a start has been made, the courts may find that

*From *The Petitioners*, by Loren Miller. Excerpts from pp. 350–356. Footnotes omitted.

additional time is necessary to carry out the ruling in an effective manner."

The ideal toward which the defendants were ordered to move was "good faith compliance at the earliest practicable date." The burden was put on the defendants to establish the need for additional time. "To that end," the Chief Justice said, "the courts may consider problems related to administration, arising from the physical condition of the school plant, the school transportation system, personnel, revision of school districts and attendance areas into compact units to achieve a system of determining admission to the public schools on a non-racial basis, and revision of local laws and regulations which may be necessary in solving the foregoing problems." The courts were ordered to enter "such orders and decrees consistent with this opinion as are necessary and proper to admit to public schools on a racially non-discriminatory basis with all deliberate speed the parties to these cases."

If the Court's order seems in the retrospect of ten years to be steeped in judicial naïveté, in light of the fact that in 1965 Negro children had been admitted to so-called white schools in less than 25 per cent of southern school districts and that not a single Negro child involved in the cases ever attended integrated schools in Clarendon County, South Carolina, or Prince Edward County, Virginia, it must be borne in mind that the Court was carried away by its own optimism in 1955. Chief Justice Warren noted with transparent pride in the second Brown decision that "substantial steps to eliminate racial discrimination in public schools have already been taken, not only in some of the communities in which these cases arose but in some of the states appearing as [friends of the Court] as well. Substantial progress has been made in the District of Columbia and in the communities in Kansas and Delaware involved in this litigation." The ink was hardly dry on the second decision before the states of the old Confederacy embarked on a program of massive resistance to the Brown decision. Compliance was orderly and meaningful only in the border states and in northern and western states with permissive segregation statutes.

The harsh truth is that the first Brown decision was a great decision; the second Brown decision was a great mistake. In the 1954 case, the Court said unequivocally that segregation of Negro children in public schools deprived them "of the equal protection of the laws guaranteed by the Fourteenth Amendment." As it had said so many times and with so much emphasis, a constitutional right is always *personal and present.* It inheres in the individual, in the *person* in constitutional language. But in the 1955 case, the Court held that a *personal and present* constitutional right could be deferred and extended gradually to those who were entitled to exercise it by virtue of a constitutional amendment. There was no constitutional warrant for such a ruling. . . .

The great vice of the Plessy case lay in the fact that the Court was induced to rule that the Constitution as amended recognized racial distinctions; the corollary was that the Negro could exercise commonplace rights and privileges, vouchsafed by birth to white persons, such as using *public* parks, playgrounds, and libraries, attending *public* schools or enjoying full use of *public* utilities such as trains or boats at the *sufferance* of the white majority. The Negro was not a *free man;* he was a *freedman,* to whom rights could be doled out by those who had set him free. (The vulgar expression of this notion is reflected in commonly heard complaints that the Negro is "moving too fast" or "demanding too much" when he seeks to exercise the same rights enjoyed as a matter of course by the white complainant.)

The Court readily saw the incongruity of requests that it defer exercise of the constitutional rights it found existent in the graduate and professional school cases, and rejected those requests out of hand by reiterating the truism that a constitutional right is always *personal and present.* No American lawyer anywhere had ever supposed that the Supreme Court, or any other organ of government, could suspend the exercise of a peacetime constitutional right for a single day. The reason is simple: a constitutional right which is not exercised at the moment of the possessor's desire is forever lost. . . .

When the Court temporized in the 1955 Brown decision and devised the deliberate-speed formula, it did so out of the best of motives. It was acting out its traditional role as the guardian of Negro rights and was moved by the triple belief—hope may be a better word—that a prompt start would be made toward compliance, that the federal district courts would act with firmness and dispatch, and that the entire process would take only a short time. No doubt it wanted to assuage the white South. It was wrong on all scores; it only succeeded in opening a Pandora's box of troubles.

The deliberate-speed formula was not only a constitutional blunder but also a practical mistake of the first order. It armed the recalcitrant states with a built-in device for delay and resistance, and actually suggested delay in some quarters. The disposition of the four state cases after the Court had devised the formula was prophetic. . . .

Only in the special case of the District of Columbia were the schools quickly desegregated. Fortunately, the District acted prior to the 1955 decision.

Of course, the Brown cases were binding only on the litigants before the Court. That is true in any case, but men of good judgment do not wait until their own conduct is condemned when they live under a government of laws and the course they have been pursuing is identical with that proscribed by the courts in another case. They put their own houses in order and thus ward off litigation. The border states of Oklahoma, Missouri, Kentucky, West Virginia, and Maryland did just that, as did the western states where segregation was permissive. But as we have seen in the peonage, confession, jury, and white primary cases, the states of the old Confederacy have never pursued any such policy in the area of civil rights. They have always depended on obstruction and defiance to preserve their old ways. They clung to that course as far as schools were concerned and waited for lawsuits, district by district, while they devised obstructionist laws and procedures. As a first step, Negroes had to apply for admission to public schools and, when refused, had to appeal to school boards for desegregation plans. If the boards refused to act, as many did, or drew up inadequate plans which were little more than legal jests, as many were, the offended Negroes had to file suit either to force the boards to act or to submit desegregation plans that were meaningful. The tragic inadequacies of the deliberate-speed formula were soon apparent.

As deliberative bodies, school boards could, and most of them did, stall for time under the pretext of considering the factors the Court had said were relevant. After they had consumed as much time as they felt was possible, their only duty was to devise a plan for desegregation. Most of the plans were shams; boards concocted evasive devices of almost every conceivable kind. Some proposed to begin with the first grade and integrate a grade a year; others offered to begin with the high schools and descend downward at the rate of a grade a year; there were proposals to integrate high schools over long periods of time and then grade schools over similar periods, or to begin with grade schools and then to proceed with high schools; elaborate pupil placement plans, fashioned to permit and conceal segregation, were presented; selective procedures were devised to prevent Negro attendance at white schools or to keep it on a token basis, or boards announced solemnly that they could do nothing because no plan could muster a majority. Legislatures entered the fray and enacted laws subtly or openly penalizing boards that did comply or other laws withdrawing state subsidies where Negro attendance occurred, or other statutes studded with procedural hurdles. Recalcitrant boards then hid behind these laws to excuse their inaction.

If a school board presented an inadequate plan or refused to present any plan, the only recourse was to file suit in a federal district court. What happened then was dependent on the good faith and temperament of the district judge. If he was hostile to the Brown decision, he could vent his hostility by taking his own good time to set and hold hearings. Many did. After such a hearing, he could approve an obviously inadequate plan. In that event the complainants could only undertake a long and arduous appeal. Many conscientious judges who disapproved the Brown decision honored their oaths and rejected inadequate plans, only to have the boards appeal and kill more time. Meanwhile, Negro children supposedly vested with a *constitutional* right to attend a public school without restriction because of race were shunted off to Jim Crow schools. By 1965, statistics showed that 2.3 per cent of southern school students were attending desegregated schools. But that figure is misleading; in many districts there was only token attendance, with most Negroes still walled off in separate schools. There was little speed in the deliberate-speed formula. The nation had reaped the fruit of the Court's refusal to declare the right to attend a public school personal and present, as it certainly was.

This is not to say that there would have been no resistance and delay had the Court not devised the deliberate-speed formula. Obviously, there would have been. Nor it is to argue that there would not have been violence, or even bloodshed, one of the evils the Court wanted to avoid. But there was violence, even bloodshed, in any event: in Little Rock; New Orleans; Oxford, Mississippi; Clinton, Tennessee. But if the Court had declared the rights of the litigants in the Brown case to have been personal and present, southern school boards could not have taken refuge in stultifying study and deliberation to clog compliance. They would have been confronted with having to make an immediate decision of either complying with the law as the Court had declared it or of facing the alternative of a lawsuit in which the only question could have been the bald issue of whether or not they had denied admission because of race or color.

The district judge before whom such a suit was presented would have had a single question for determination: Was, or was not, the denial of admission based on race or color? He could then have issued the proper writ of mandate or injunction ordering or denying admission.

WOW

KNOW THIS POINT

He would not have had to study an elaborate "plan" or to devise one himself. True enough, he could have dragged his feet in setting the case for trial or in rendering a decision. But he could not have gone beyond that. On appeal by either side, the courts of appeals would not have had to restudy the "plan" offered by a school board or devised by the district judge, or to devise new plans; they, too, would have been confronted with a single issue. Where ingenious defenses were offered, the district judge or the judges of the courts of appeal would have been assisted by the Supreme Court's rule that the Constitution dooms "ingenious as well as simple minded modes of discrimination."

In shying away from declaring the rights sought in the Brown case to be personal and present, the Court was also undoubtedly moved by the belief that the gradualistic approach would be less offensive and more readily acceptable to the South. The sober truth is that change would have been gradual in any event. Negroes habituated to segregation would have moved slowly. As the chosen instrument of Negroes seeking change, the NAACP lacked financial resources and manpower to proceed in any other than a gradual manner, district by district, where boards of education did not act on application of Negroes. It could have, and undoubtedly would have, acted with as much dispatch as possible, but it could not have wrought a revolution. Armed, as they should have been, with a declaration that the right imbedded in the Fourteenth Amendment was personal and present, Negroes could have secured the claimed right at a much faster pace for the good of Negro children—and for the nation.

wow

JACK GREENBERG (b. 1924) has been Director-Counsel of the NAACP Legal Defense and Educational Fund since 1961. He replaced Thurgood Marshall when Marshall was appointed to the Federal District Court. Greenberg is the author of *Race Relations and American Law* (1959). In the fine, scholarly article below, Greenberg examines the policy interrelationships of Supreme Court enforcement of *Brown* and the decisions on protest demonstrations. He sees the Court in this period primarily as teacher. Until the mid-1960s, it taught that racial discrimination was wrong and unconstitutional by enunciating general principles, while waiting for the forces of political change to gain momentum. But it reversed convictions of civil rights demonstrators who were also "teaching" the country about racial discrimination. After the Civil Rights Act of 1964, the Court became more active in pressing for integration; at the same time it let convictions stand, apparently out of uneasiness over the growing level of social tension.*

Jack Greenberg

Civil Rights and Militant Protest: The Court as Teacher[1]

Because it has the power to affect broad currents of American thought and behavior, the Supreme Court must of necessity operate with some consciousness of the social effects of its determinations. The synthesizing of precedent and the interpretation of statutes and of the Constitution are of course the stuff of day-to-day decision-making. But such considerations as the capacity of legal pronouncements to teach certain principles, the power of the courts to compel desirable conduct, and the possibility that particular rulings will reinforce or weaken obedience to the law can, in appropriate cases, exercise considerable influence upon Court determinations. Such considerations, to be sure, seldom manifest themselves on the surface of decisions in which they play a role. The Justices themselves—or some of them—may not be aware of certain unarticulated premises underlying their decisions in a

[1] This article is based on the 1966 Meiklejohn Lecture at Brown University. The reader should note that I have been counsel in many of the cases cited herein, which has perhaps given some insight at the risk of impairing vision in other respects.

*Jack Greenberg, "The Supreme Court, Civil Rights and Civil Dissonance." Reprinted by permission of the Yale Law Journal Company and Fred B. Rothman & Company from *The Yale Law Journal,* Vol. 77, pp. 1520–1541 (July 1968).

given case or line of cases. In addition, the popular belief that social policy should not be weighed in deciding particular cases contributes to judicial reticence to acknowledge such considerations. More important, perhaps, there is frequently no need to articulate important policies behind a decision if the Justices choose not to do so. Much of the Court's policy-making is accomplished by simple grant and denial of certiorari, grounds for which are rarely set forth. . . . Their existence must be inferred from patterns of decision over a period of years, by comparison and contrast of the Court's varying treatments of related lines of cases.

The civil rights movement has given rise to a number of important lines of Supreme Court decisions which illustrate the influence of such unarticulated policy considerations. Two of these—the school desegregation and protest demonstration cases—have recently completed phases of development. The school cases have passed from a period in which the Court limited itself to the enunciation of general principles of educational equality, to one in which the Court has shown an increasing willingness to involve itself in details of desegregation plans. The pattern followed by the protest cases has been nearly the opposite. From a period of detailed review of sit-in convictions, accompanied almost invariably by reversal on narrow grounds, the Court has progressed to a point where it frequently leaves the last word to the states in protest demonstration cases, sometimes affirming with broad pronouncements on public order and property rights.

These changing patterns of Court decision have paralleled other legal and social developments. In the school desegregation area passage of the Civil Rights Act of 1964, made possible in significant degree by the demonstrations which were part of the heritage of *Brown* v. *Board of Education,* has resulted in the supplementing of private-suit enforcement of desegregation by federal enforcement under Title VI of the Act. In the protest demonstration area the last eight years have seen a progression from the nonviolent 1960 Greensboro sit-ins through the Selma march of 1965 to a period of widespread social protest. In recent years civil rights protests have been joined in national prominence by other demonstrations such as those against the war in Viet Nam, or the student uprisings at Berkeley and Columbia. During the same period the country has been shocked by the summer riots which have wracked our cities. And although the early civil rights demonstrations and much of the protest which has succeeded them have differed in participants, purposes, methods and legality, there has been an easy tendency to lump together the growing civil dissonance[2] as a single phenomenon.

It is not fortuitous that the school desegregation and sit-in lines of decision have developed as they have. I suggest that the patterns of social development

[2] My meaning is more clearly expressed by the term "civil dissonance" than by the more common "civil disobedience." Civil disobedience connotes illegal conduct pursued out of political motives, but much protest that has been called "civilly disobedient," even by the actors themselves, has in fact been legal. Violation of a local law which is in conflict with the Constitution or federal law (*e.g.*, freedom rides) is not civilly disobedient, because the Constitution validates the conduct in question: the local law is invalid. Moreover, action giving rise to test case litigation ought not to be viewed as civil disobedience. Those engaged in lunch counter sit-ins, for example, even if they had not been ultimately upheld by the courts and Congress, arguably believed that they had a Fourteenth Amendment right to sit-in. At least three Justices of the Supreme Court agreed with them. *Bell* v. *Maryland,* 378 U.S. 226, 286 (1964).

outlined above are interrelated with one another; that there are connections between the early school decision rhetoric, the sit-in demonstrations, the early reversals of sit-in convictions, the Civil Rights Act, the spreading civil dissonance and the Court's recent tendency to let protest convictions stand. I suggest, furthermore, that those connections can perhaps best be understood in terms of the Court's—and the law's—role as a teacher.

On the one hand the Court can teach by the direct advocacy of ideas, by the eloquent and forceful declaration of principles it holds dear. On the other it can "teach" by approving or condemning certain conduct. In either case the ultimate goal is the encouragement of desired forms of thought and behavior. The school desegregation cases were in this sense far more than enforceable judgments. Indeed for almost ten years enforcement was perhaps their least important aspect. The opinions proclaimed for the first time from the summit of one of the three branches of the federal government the immorality as well as the illegality of segregation. The early protest decisions were also more than simply enforceable judgments. In ultimate effect they were intimately related to the school decisions, protecting a movement that was forcefully teaching the American people the same lessons that the school decisions had abstractly taught.

Brown v. *Board of Education* proved to be the Declaration of Independence of its day. Together with the other school desegregation cases it profoundly affected national thinking and has served as the principal ideological engine of today's civil rights movement. Without announcing any radically new ideas, it nevertheless helped to crystallize a national commitment to eradicate racial inequality. To a nation which had recently fought a war against Nazism and its doctrines of racial inferiority, to a nation whose regional, educational and social barriers were being threatened and in some cases breached and overthrown by advances in communication and transportation, to a nation whose Negroes, together with its other citizens, had begun to enjoy the benefits of a higher level of prosperity and to hunger for more, the Court said that this is not a nation which may sort out people on the basis of race.

Thus *Brown* forcefully and authoritatively proclaimed an ideal. But the decision, because it was a decision of the Court, had a force that ordinary speech cannot have. While ordinary speech cannot require a response, a lawyer could put the *Brown* holding into the machinery of the legal process and bring about confrontations demanding some sort of answers. In Atlanta, Birmingham, Nashville, Little Rock, New Orleans—indeed in every large and medium-size city in the South as well as in more than a hundred rural counties, lawyers filed suits requesting the enforcement of rights assured or suggested by the Brown decision. The resulting discussion among lawyers, judges, academics and leading private citizens—through press, radio, television and direct confrontation—made important breaches in the class, ethnic and other barriers which belie the popular image of America as one great "melting pot." Lawsuits created a dialogue between leaders of the Negro and white communities. The legal process drew both sides into a single arena and made them deal with well-defined issues. In addition, suits stimulated informal discussions between the parties that until then had been taboo. Desegregation, though often limited and sometimes of token nature, introduced new living experiences to private citizens and public officials as well.

The stimulation of this great national dialogue was for many years, however, the extent of the Supreme Court's involvement in the school desegregation struggle. While repeatedly and unequivocally asserting as a general proposition that school boards must desegregate and must do so promptly, the Court refrained from involving itself in the details of the implementation process and until recently has assumed jurisdiction only on occasions when a large issue of principle was at stake.

The second *Brown* opinion was the first opportunity for the Court to discuss implementation. As in the earlier decision, the Court confined itself to laying down general principles. Despite the abuse that has been heaped on the opinion's "deliberate speed" formula, however, the Court did state the basic requirements of school desegregation in unequivocal terms. Hostility was ruled out as a ground for delay; the entire *system* had to be desegregated; only practical administrative considerations could justify anything less. If school boards had followed the lead of *Brown II*, the nation's schools would have been desegregated in a few years. Whatever blame is assignable to the 1955 opinion for the slow pace that actually followed must be charged to its tone, which in the context of the widespread assumption that desegregation would have to be accomplished instantaneously was taken by many school boards to indicate judicial reluctance to upset the status quo.

Between 1955 and 1958, the year of the Little Rock case,[3] the Court did not discuss school segregation at all. It merely declined to review cases. The Little Rock case was an occasion for reaffirmation of principle. The Court not only endorsed the substantive portions of *Brown*, but took the unique step of asserting that each and every member of the Court, including those Justices who had ascended to the bench following *Brown*, agreed in "unanimously reaffirm[ing]" the earlier opinion. Nothing less was required to demonstrate that the political opposition to *Brown* would not move the Court to retract or modify it. Again the opinion was notable chiefly for its broad-brushed enunciation of principle. It began with the stern warning that "[a]s this case reaches us it raises questions of the highest importance to the maintenance of our federal system of government." The Court reviewed at some length and in somewhat more specific terms the standards established by *Brown II*, reasserting the need for expedition in desegregating. Almost nothing, however, was said about the details or method of desegregation in Little Rock, nor about its pace. . . .

From 1958 to 1963, with few exceptions, the Court continued to refuse to review school cases, whether brought up by plaintiffs or by defendant school boards. The exceptional cases it did review followed the established pattern of emphasizing principle and avoiding the specifics of implementation. . . .

The Civil Rights Act of 1964 marked a watershed in the Court's treatment of school desegregation cases. In the 1965 term three school cases were decided. Two of them, *Bradley* v. *School Board* and *Gilliam* v. *School Board*, marked a limited departure from the earlier pattern of decisions. They held that plaintiffs were entitled to hearings on the impact of teacher segregation on the desegregation process, adding . . . that "[d]elays in

---

[3] *Cooper* v. *Aaron*.

desegregation of school systems are no longer tolerable." *Gilliam* also refused to discuss a gerrymandering question raised in the petition for certiorari.

The third decision, however, manifested a distinct change in the Court's willingness to grapple with details of enforcement in school cases. *Rogers* v. *Paul,* after quoting the *Bradley* principle that "[d]elays in desegregating public school systems are no longer tolerable," ordered prompt admission of Negro children to a high school from which they had been excluded because the district's gradual desegregation plan had not reached their grades:

> Pending the desegregation of the public high schools of Fort Smith according to a general plan consistent with this principle, petitioner and those similarly situated shall be allowed immediate transfer to the high school that has the more extensive curriculum and from which they are excluded because of their race.

. . . In May of this year [1968] . . . three further decisions examined whether certain "freedom of choice" plans fulfilled the Board's "affirmative duty to take whatever steps might be necessary to convert [the state-imposed dual school system] to a unitary system in which racial discrimination would be eliminated root and branch." *Green, Monroe* and *Raney* all emphasized that they were striking down the challenged plans *as applied,* not in the abstract, and *Green* and *Raney* took the further step of suggesting specifically that geographical zoning might serve as the basis for acceptable plans. The Court has clearly moved away from its pre-Civil Rights Act role as an exponent of guiding principles alone to a more active involvement in the particulars of school desegregation.

The role played by the Supreme Court in the sit-in cases produced by the civil rights demonstrations of the early 1960's was precisely the reverse of its approach in the school cases. Between 1961 and 1965 the Court passed on the merits of more than 30 sit-in prosecutions for entering upon or refusing to leave privately owned public accommodations—usually restaurants—which excluded or segregated Negroes. Demonstrators were typically prosecuted for trespass, breach of the peace and similar crimes, and were defended on the grounds that the state was suppressing free speech and enforcing racial discrimination in violation of the First and Fourteenth Amendments. The protestors won virtually all of their cases in the Supreme Court. Almost invariably, however, the Court's decisions rested on the narrowest possible grounds, without reaching the basic constitutional issues involved.

The pattern of decision is highly unusual if the cases are viewed in isolation as so many trespass, breach of the peace, disorderly conduct and weight of evidence cases. It is unheard of for the Supreme Court, which can decide only a relatively small number of cases each term, to repeatedly take up such apparently minor matters. Viewed in the context of race relations in the United States, however, the Court's constant involvement can be understood as reflecting concern that a nonviolent movement, struggling toward the same goals that the Court itself had urged more abstractly on the nation in the early school desegregation decisions, should not be worn down by petty prosecutions. . . .

In 1961 the Court decided the first three sit-in cases to arise out of actual demonstrations. . . . Plaintiffs argued that there was no evidence to sustain their convictions, that they were engaged in constitutionally protected free speech, and that they enjoyed Fourteenth Amendment immunity from prosecution for violating segregation rules of private managers of public accommodations. The Court reversed on the ground that the record contained no evidence that defendants had disturbed the peace, a decision of little or no meaning in doctrinal terms. But to the young people in the movement it suggested that courts would protect them. The movement was encouraged.

In 1963 the Court decided another series of sit-in cases. These arose in Greenville, Birmingham, Durham and New Orleans. Greenville, Birmingham and Durham had city ordinances requiring racial segregation in public accommodations. The Court again declined to pass upon broad First and Fourteenth Amendment claims, but held that the segregation complained of was not private discrimination, because segregation at lunch counters was required by ordinance in those cities. The convictions were therefore invalid under the Equal Protection Clause as enforcement of governmentally required discrimination. New Orleans had no city ordinance requiring segregation, but the mayor and police chief had publicly declared that sit-in demonstrations would not be tolerated. The Court treated this as equivalent to an ordinance requiring segregation and reversed. Once more a series of decisions on limited grounds made no great new constitutional doctrine but nevertheless protected the demonstrators. . . .

Throughout this period the vagueness doctrine, which weaves pervasively through free speech law, was employed by the Court as another limited ground of disposition in demonstration cases. The requirement that laws be precise enough so that local officials cannot distort them to suppress unpopular views found frequent application in cases involving common law breach of the peace and similar amorphous offenses. In *Edwards* v. *South Carolina* the Court reversed a series of convictions for peaceful assembly and parading on the statehouse grounds; it held that the common law breach of the peace doctrine under which defendants had been convicted was so general and vague that it allowed unconstitutional infringement of their First Amendments rights.

Bell v. *Maryland,* decided on June 22, 1964, marked the beginning of the end for prosecutions of sit-in demonstrators. After the Maryland Court of Appeals had affirmed the conviction, but while the case was still pending on writ of certiorari before the Supreme Court, Maryland passed its own state civil rights law, making it unlawful for restaurants to deny service to any person because of his race. Noting the new state law, the Court pointed to the ancient common law doctrine of "abatement," which states that if the reason for punishment ceases while a case is still in the courts, punishment ought not to be inflicted. Since it thought that the Maryland courts might apply such a rule to the *Bell* case, the Court sent the case back for reconsideration. The Court was also aware that Congress was less than two weeks from passing a national public accommodations act, Title II of the Civil Rights Act of 1964. It did not take much imagination to predict that the federal law might similarly affect convictions all over the country.

Indeed the principal argument of defendants in *Hamm* v. *City of Rock Hill* and *Lupper* v. *Arkansas,* cases decided in December of the same year, was that the 1964 Civil Rights Act abated sit-in convictions based on acts which could not have been prosecuted if performed after the passage of the statute. The Supreme

Court agreed and held the convictions abated. The law the sit-inners had helped to create protected them. Today occasional pre-1964 sit-in cases continue to be decided in the lower courts, usually being disposed of on the basis of abatement.

Thus in contrast to the pattern of decision in the school desegregation cases, the sit-in decisions were characterized by wholesale granting of certiorari and by studious avoidance of the broad constitutional issues underlying the details of particular cases. The ad hoc character of the decisions, however, did not interfere with consistent results. In case after case a majority of the Court consistently upheld the protesters. The petitioners whose convictions were overturned were, to be sure, often model defendants. Their demonstrations had invariably been nonviolent; they pointed up extreme injustice by emphasizing, for example, the unfairness of segregated lunch counters in stores which did not object in the least to selling merchandise to anyone who could pay; the demonstrators usually had no way of securing desegregation through the courts, and even where that was in theory possible, litigation would have been lengthy and expensive. Congress and state legislatures were, at the outset of the demonstration movement, unresponsive, and state officials were frequently unnecessarily ruthless in policing and prosecuting the demonstrators. When these factors combined, many of the rules of law that protect defendants in criminal cases, secure equality to victims of racial discrimination, and protect speech seemed to operate at maximum potential.

Nevertheless, considerations militating against approval of many of the protests were never far beneath the surface. The possibility of violence lurked in many situations. Various Justices in dissents expressed disquiet about the physical encounters that even peaceful protestors might provoke by their demonstrations. In addition, the concept of private property—which in the sit-in cases, of course, begged the question of whether there is a property right under the Fourteenth Amendment to exclude Negroes from privately owned public places—exerts a powerful emotional influence. And the two considerations—fear of violence and attachment to property rights—reinforce one another because some individuals are quick to employ violence to protect their property. Finally, there was the uneasy feeling that the protestors' exhortation to disobey unjust, or even unconstitutional, laws would encourage disobedience of law in general.

Thus when, as the demonstrations filled out their first half decade, nonviolent civil rights demonstrations were joined by more violent forms of protest and by protests ranging far beyond civil rights, it was not surprising that a reaction set in. Nor was it surprising that the outbreak of urban rioting—unconnected to the civil rights movement except that both were fueled by the same injustices—should be uncritically lumped with the other forms of civil dissonance. . . .

Between 1964 and 1967 the public protest cases coming to the Court less frequently involved protest against racial discrimination and more often involved disorder. And the Court's refusals to review convictions proliferated. When the Court did grant certiorari, its opinions increasingly manifested the concern that earlier dissents had displayed, implicitly and explicitly, towards the rising level of dissonance in the country. . . .

Conspicuous among refusals to hear was the five-to-four dismissal of certiorari as improvidently granted in *NAACP*

v. *Overstreet* the following year. The case posed the issue whether Georgia courts could make the national organization liable for acts committed by a local branch. The dissenters observed: "Although the record does not contain any evidence of misconduct on the part of the Branch's members or officers, the picketing apparently attracted substantial crowds. There were incidents involving the intimidation of customers, blocking of sidewalks, and scattered incidents of violence."

In 1967 the Court, in *McLaurin* v. *Greenville,* made a similar silent disposition, denying certiorari in the case of a group of civil rights workers who made speeches on the Greenville courthouse steps and were prosecuted under a state statute identical to the one the Court had previously struck down . . . as unconstitutionally vague on its face. The Mississippi Supreme Court's decision observed that "there was a clear and present danger of a riot or disturbance of court then in session. . ." It is difficult to put aside the feeling that if the case had come up three or four years earlier with *Edwards* v. *South Carolina* . . . it would have been difficult to distinguish among them and the judgment would have been reversed. And during the October 1966 Term, a majority for the first time by affirmance of convictions turned its face against civil rights demonstrators in two important cases, *Adderly* v. *Florida* and *Walker* v. *City of Birmingham*. . . .

Adderley, in which Justices Black, Clark, Harlan, Stewart and White constituted the majority, involved a charge of trespass arising out of a protest against the arrest of students who were imprisoned at the Tallahassee, Florida, jail. On its facts the case was much like *Edwards* (in which Justice Stewart had written the opinion with only Justice Clark dissenting) except that the demonstration took place on jail property, not statehouse grounds, and defendants were charged under a trespass statute, not with common law breach of the peace. These were the articulated differences. But the most significant distinction may very well be that *Adderley* was decided in November 1966 at a time when the dissonance of demonstrations of all sorts had reached a new high. Justice Black's *Adderley* majority opinion went to great lengths to emphasize the impromptu and disorganized nature of the protest, the size of the crowd, and the demonstrators' interference with passage to and from the jail. . . .

During the same term of the Court, *Walker* v. *City of Birmingham* (in which Justice Stewart wrote the opinion for the same majority as in *Adderley*) upheld the contempt conviction of the Reverend Martin Luther King, Jr., and others for having violated an injunction forbidding the celebrated Good Friday and Easter Sunday Birmingham marches that were crucial to the demonstrations which led to passage of the 1964 Civil Rights Act. Some of the tone and language of the *Walker* opinion is reminiscent of demonstration case dissents several years earlier. The Alabama court held that petitioners owed obedience to the injunction and should have moved to dissolve it before disobeying it, even though it may have been unconstitutional. The Supreme Court declined to pass on the validity of the injunction, holding that the only question before it was whether the court order had in fact been disobeyed. The entire sense of the opinion is to value order and orderly judicial procedure over speech, even if that speech is suppressed in violation of the First and Fourteenth Amendments:

The rule of law that Alabama followed in this case reflects a belief that in the fair administration of justice no man can be judge in his own case, however exalted his station, however righteous his motives, and irrespective of his race, color, politics, or religion. This Court cannot hold that the petitioners were constitutionally free to ignore all the procedures of the law and carry their battle to the streets. . . .

Justice Brennon, in dissent, made no effort to conceal his belief that the majority's overriding concern with public order had warped its perception of the issues involved.

We cannot permit fears of "riots" and "civil disobedience" generated by slogans like "Black Power" to divert our attention from what is here at stake—not violence or the right of the State to control its streets and sidewalks, but the insulation from attack of ex parte orders and legislation upon which they are based even when patently impermissible prior restraints on the exercise of the First Amendment rights. . . .

But precisely such fears *were* diverting the Court's attention, and many of its decisions against demonstrators reflect the effects of its concern.

The early school decisions with their attention to principles and avoidance of specifics, principally served the purposes of educating the country and making clear that defiance could not succeed, rather than of compelling action by particular parties. Ultimately, of course, *Brown* implied a power to compel change; it would have been useless as a national guide if that were not so. But no move was made by the Court toward implementation of the kind found repeatedly in the reapportionment cases, to mention only one example.

Several reasons may be suggested for the Court's reluctance to grapple with detail in the school cases. The Court was, in the early cases, chiefly setting standards for the lower courts, where the great bulk of litigation went on. Apart from the uninviting prospect of repeated involvement in the intricacies of school desegregation, it may be that the Court spoke in generalities and avoided details because its determinations could be of only limited utility in the overall desegregation process. The principal reason for the slow pace of school desegregation before 1964 was not, after all, inattention to detail or the "deliberate speed" formula. Rather, it was the failure of most deep southern districts to do anything at all. The typical district would start desegregation only if sued. Since the 1964 Civil Rights Act had not yet been passed, there was no authority in the federal government to bring suit and no administrative mechanism to compel change; and the resources to bring private suit were limited. . . . As a practical matter, therefore, the Court chose to exert its influence through strong moral leadership.

With the passage of the 1964 Civil Rights Act and the vesting of authority to implement *Brown* in HEW and the Justice Department, however, the practical significance of a Supreme Court school desegregation decision changed considerably. Uniformity became possible for the first time. Since it was now far less likely that a district would be compelled to comply while its neighbors remained in violation, one incentive to delay desegregation in hopes of escaping altogether was removed. Most important, HEW enforces guidelines embodying a distillation of judicial opinion. To the extent that the Court upgrades specific standards, they are then capable of widespread enforcement by an agency with potentially large staff and appropriations, although the funding and vigor of the HEW enforcement staff are subject to political considerations. In addition the Department of Justice, aided by the investigative power of the Federal Bureau of Investigation, has begun to take a more active part in school desegregation. The role of private suits in the school area is changing back to what it was before *Brown,* to innovating and pushing forward in situations where government for one reason or another does not.

Another consideration which may have inclined the Court to avoid involvement in a multitude of school desegregation cases was that until the Civil Rights Act was passed the country had not yet shown that it endorsed the position taken by the Supreme Court in the first school cases. President Eisenhower, for one, explicitly refused to approve of them. While all civil liberties decisions are by definition to some degree unpopular—there would be little need for judicial relief if political remedies were readily available—the *Brown* decision, especially in some parts of the country, was more unpopular than most. It affected a large part of the nation, invited opposition by powerful southern politicians, and brought down a storm of invective on the Court. Negroes at the time of *Brown* were substantially disenfranchised in the region it affected most. And the Court came close to suffering, through Congressional legislation, heavy damage to its jurisdiction. . . . The Court's limiting of its role in the early school desegregation cases to enunciation of fundamental principles may well have reflected its estimation of the most effective and prudent course open to it. Once passage of the Civil Rights Act of 1964 signalled that the rest of the country had at last caught up, however, the Court could feel free to involve itself more intimately in necessary implementation.

In contrast to its approach in the school suits, in the protest demonstration area the Court did not shy away from repeatedly weighing the particulars of complex fact situations. It did this, moreover, in a style unlike that of the school suits by normally avoiding expansive constitutional pronouncements. This had, to begin with, the effect of leaving the Court's options open for later cases, in which it refused to review the claims of petitioners in other kinds of demonstrations. It was one thing to refuse to hear narrow evidentiary arguments or claims concerning procedure or vagueness; it would have been quite another to refuse for any length of time to hear cases involving recently delimited First or Fourteenth Amendment rights.

In part, cases may have gone off so narrowly because general propositions governing the right to demonstrate cannot be stated as simply as general propositions governing the right to desegregated education. Whether there is a Fourteenth Amendment right to sit in a privately owned public restaurant, or a Commerce Clause immunity from arrest for trespass at a bus terminal lunch counter, is a far more complex and difficult question than those raised by the post-*Brown* school cases. Avoidance has been a natural response.

But if that is the case, why did the Court grant review at all? Ordinarily the Court does not review minor criminal cases involving limited issues. Indeed, most defendants convicted of trespass, breach of the peace and similar crimes simply pay their small fines or serve their brief sentences and let the matter drop. Certainly the Court, having once decided the narrow issues to which it confined itself, would not have ruled on them repeatedly if something more were not involved, if the cases had not been "important" in the sense that merits granting of review. The fact that the cases came up in such volume at all was of course in one sense an index of importance. . . . Apart from their consequences for particular defendants and for the civil rights movement, the reversals meant something for the education of the country. The Court has long recognized the "chilling" effect of pending criminal prosecutions on speech. One might analogously describe the Court's repeated reversals of protest demonstration convictions as having a "thawing" effect.

The cumulative effect of the sit-in reversals no doubt was to encourage the demonstrators to continue their activities. . . . Demonstrators were less likely to be intimidated by fear of conviction. Those who otherwise might have remained in jail were free to protest elsewhere. The consistent reversals gave an implicit stamp of approval to the cause espoused by the demonstrators and allowed them to work toward realization of ideals embraced by the Court itself in *Brown*.

Less certain is the relationship between the Court's recent pattern of disposition of protest cases and the increased dissonance of public protest generally. But the coincidence suggests that the affirmance of convictions and general indisposition to grant review in demonstration cases may be an effort to retard or undo supposed effects of the earlier thaw and to allow the states to reimpose a freeze. . . .

If recent Court decisions in the civil rights area have been in part a reaction to the rising tide of civil dissonance on other fronts, the question remains whether such a reaction is either logical or likely to produce the desired results. No one, of course, can be sure of the causal relationships among the various forms of protest. Whether the nonviolent civil rights demonstrations that were legal or intended to be tests of legality led to those which went clearly beyond legal bounds is a question which must be left to the social psychologists. The relationships between civil rights protests and public demonstrations on other issues, such as student-university relationships or the war in Viet Nam, is again something about which we cannot be sure. But it is hard to believe that if there had been no Birmingham or Selma we would have avoided Berkeley and Columbia or the recent confrontation at the Pentagon.

Even if we assume that legal protest contributed to wider dissonance and civil disobedience, will curtailing the scope of legal protest turn the clock back? Is this a two-way or a one-way street? More importantly, will judicial reluctance or refusal to upset convictions based on irregular modes of prosecution promote public tranquility, or will it instead weaken respect for law and law enforcement?

A prominent and prolific writer on the recent period of Supreme Court history, ALEXANDER M. BICKEL (b. 1924) has been professor of law at Yale since 1960. In studies such as *The Least Dangerous Branch: The Supreme Court at the Bar of Politics* (1962), he has generally taken the "judicial restraint" position advocated by Justice Felix Frankfurter. This position argues for caution and subtlety by the Court in achieving its policy objectives as well as for deference to the wishes of popularly elected legislatures. His *Supreme Court and the Idea of Progress* (1969), from which this selection is taken, is a critique of several aspects of the Warren Court. Bickel maintains that the Court's *Brown* decision was motivated in part by the ideal of the integrated public school as the matrix of democracy. This objective is likely to fail, he holds. Although the problems of integration are many and persistent, one wonders if Bickel's subtlety has not overreached itself. Has he set up a straw man in respect to the intentions of *Brown* and then knocked that straw man down?*

Alexander M. Bickel

A Pessimistic View: Brown *May Be Irrelevant*

At the first argument of *Brown* v. *Board of Education* in 1952, Justice Frankfurter asked the future Justice Thurgood Marshall, then counsel for the Negro children, whether a decision in his favor would "entitle every mother to have her child go to a nonsegregated school?" Mr. Marshall replied in the negative. "What will it do?" Justice Frankfurter pursued. Mr. Marshall replied: "The school board, I assume, would find some other method of distributing the children by drawing district lines." The only requirement would be, Mr. Marshall added, that the lines be drawn "on a natural basis," and not be gerrymandered so as to enclose or exclude Negro neighborhoods.

It has not been that simple. It has not been that simple because for a decade resistance to any desegregation, of any sort, in any measure, was fierce and uncompromising in much of the South, and even now many districts are yielding only grudgingly, and must still be pushed step by step. It has not been that simple also

*Abridged from pp. 117–120, 126–133, 140–142, 150–151, in *The Supreme Court and the Idea of Progress* by Alexander M. Bickel. Copyright © 1970 by Alexander M. Bickel. Reprinted by permission of Harper & Row, Publishers, Inc. Footnotes omitted.

because the laconic opinion in *Brown* v. *Board of Education* was itself not that simple. One strain in it became evident in subsequent decisions outlawing all forms of state-sponsored segregation in everything from the spectator section of a courtroom to golf courses. The minimal proposition that emerged—and about time it was that it should emerge—was that the state may not, by legislation or administratively, classify the population along racial lines. . . .

Another element in the *Brown* decision was the Court's concern, not with race relations in general, but specifically with education. "Today," said the Court in *Brown,* "education is perhaps the most important function of state and local governments. Compulsory school attendance laws and the great expenditures for education both demonstrate our recognition of the importance of education to our democratic society. . . . It is the very foundation of good citizenship." The opportunity for an education, the Court concluded, "where the state has undertaken to provide it," is a right to be made available to all on equal terms. Separate schools did not make it so available because the black child's sense that he was classified by race induced a feeling of inferiority in him, which affected his motivation. The child's education was consequently impaired; it was unequal.

Now it is not easy to maintain the position that the impairment and the inequality result only from segregation imposed by official legislative or administrative action, and not from separation as such, however it may have come about, by official or private initiative, exercised recently or long ago. If a Negro child perceives his separation as discriminatory and invidious, he is not, in a society a hundred years removed from slavery, going to make fine distinctions about the source of a particular separation. The Court implied as much when it quoted with approval a statement by a lower-court judge to the effect that the detrimental consequences of school segregation were heightened—merely heightened—when segregation had the sanction of law.

From here it is a very short step to yet another idea, namely, that separate public schooling, whatever the cause of it, the means by which it is enforced, or its psychological impact on the individual black child, is inherently inferior for everyone concerned, because the function of the public school cannot be successfully performed unless children of all groups are taught in it together. . . .

For a decade, the conception of the function of public schools implicit in *Brown* v. *Board of Education* . . . had no bearing on the process of administering the desegregation of Southern schools. Much of the South challenged the minimal requirement of *Brown:* that segregation cease being enforced by law. Making at times dramatic use of their equity powers, the lower federal courts, with the exception of certain unsympathetic and even rebellious judges, but with the support of the Supreme Court, withstood this challenge in its many shapes. (In 1964, in the Civil Rights Act of that year, Congress came to the aid of the courts by giving legislative form to the minimal rule of the *Brown* case, and putting additional if very limited resources into its enforcement.)

When schools were closed by state authorities for the sole reason that federal courts had ordered them desegregated, the actions were held unconstitutional, and the schools in effect reopened by court decree. When state and local governments, as part of the same statutory schemes that closed public schools in order to prevent their desegregation, made available tuition grants to pupils transferring to segregated private schools, so-called, the payment of the tuition grants was forbidden—although it was somewhat curious that the courts should forbid payment of the grants rather than order the desegregation of the private schools, which they found to be thinly disguised substitutes for segregated public schools.

In the second decade of desegregation, the totally unyielding resistance of earlier years having been broken for the most part, the minimal rule of *Brown* took on some complexity, and the Warren Court's assumptions concerning the effect of segregation on the Negro child, and concerning the necessary role of public schools began to come into play, however indirectly.

The courts have been faced with token compliance, and with devices calculated to enable school boards to retain as many segregated situations as possible. Like the Department of Health, Education and Welfare in its own efforts to implement the Civil Rights Act of 1964, the courts have sometimes responded with orders that Southern school boards produce a given percentage of Negro children in desegregated schools by a given date. And since a segregated faculty characterizes a school as white or Negro, faculties have also been required to be integrated on a percentage basis.

In a series of cases decided in May, 1968, the Supreme Court said that Southern school boards must produce desegregation plans that work realistically, and "work *now.*" A plan that works, the Court made fairly clear, is a plan that does not merely free Negro children to attend white schools, but that actually results in integrated schools *now.* The Court held that in a rural district, with relatively little housing segregation, a freedom-of-choice plan, under which all pupils, white and Negro, could choose which school to attend, had not worked satisfactorily. The plan had produced not a single white child attending the formerly all-Negro school, although 115 Negro children enrolled in the formerly all-white school. Eighty-five percent of the Negro children in the district remained in the all-Negro school.

The Court's holding was tied to evidence of foot dragging and bad faith on the part of the school board. A freedom-of-choice plan implemented in good faith was not necessarily unconstitutional, the Court said, taking account, for once, of varied conditions, and tolerating some diversity. But where other courses of action, promising more desegregation, are open to the board, the Court went on, failure to take them "may indicate a lack of good faith; and at the least it places a heavy burden upon the board to explain its preference for an apparently less effective method." The Court added even more explicitly that "if there are reasonably available other ways, such for illustration as zoning, promising speedier and more effective conversion to a unitary, non-racial school system, 'freedom of choice' must be held unacceptable."

Another of the cases decided by the Supreme Court in May, 1968, arose in Jackson, Tennessee, a city of forty thousand with a school population some 40 percent Negro, which put a nonracial zoning plan into effect, but allowed free transfers of students out of their zones, limited only by the availability of space elsewhere. The result was that all whites assigned to previously Negro schools transferred out, and many Negroes transferred back to Negro schools after being assigned to previously all-white ones. Schools that were previously all-Negro remained so, even though one junior high school was fairly thoroughly integrated, as were also one or two elementary schools. The Court held that this performance was "clearly inadequate," and that the transfers must cease. But again the holding was tied to intimations of the school board's bad faith. . . .

Only in some cities have Southern conditions quite come to resemble the situation in the North and West, where there is generally no problem of segregation imposed by law. Hence, decrees in cases such as those just discussed do not in theory rest on the proposition that any sort of segregation, however arrived at, hurts the Negro child, is also otherwise inconsistent with the mission of the public schools, and is for these reasons unconstitutional; and these decrees do not expressly require racial balance in the schools. Rather, against a background of sustained resistance, they purport merely to demand the production of convincing evidence of compliance with the minimal rule that legally-imposed segregation must be disestablished. Yet, even if only for evidentiary purposes, these decrees also require more than just disestablishment, and they reflect, therefore, all the elements that entered into the decision of *Brown* v. *Board of Education,* not simply the rule that state-sponsored segregation is unconstitutional. On their face, they are informed by a conception of the mission of the public school as assimilationist—a conception that is as pertinent to the rest of the country as to the South.

Outside the South, of course, school segregation is massive, and has, indeed, increased substantially in recent years, even though it has not been established by law for many decades, but is caused mainly by residential patterns. Nevertheless, very few federal courts have tried to intervene, none has done so without qualification, and the Supreme Court has carefully refrained from becoming involved. Here and there, school authorities have been shown to have intentionally instituted or fostered segregation, and perhaps that could be shown more often than it has been. Where it has been, federal courts have issued decrees somewhat like the ones in the latest, most advanced Southern cases, but seldom otherwise. . . .

When, however, there is no reason to take the basic assumption of bad faith or of a mental reservation in favor of a segregated system, then a judge who is asked to modify decisions about districting, or site selection, or tracking of pupils, or failure to bus, or failure to close a school, or failure to pair two schools, or to consolidate one or more grades in a central school—a judge asked to review and reverse such decisions is then in a position of simply remaking educational and other local policy. He must either be able to convince himself that the goal of integration overrides all others and that the schools must discharge their assimilationist mission at all costs, regardless of other considerations, or he must have uncommon confidence in his own capacity as an educational policy maker.

But that is not the worst of it. In most of the larger urban areas, demographic conditions are such that no policy that a court can order, and a school board, a city, or even a state has the capability to put into effect, will in fact result in the foreseeable future in racially balanced public schools. Only a reordering of the environment involving economic and social policy on the broadest conceivable front might have an appreciable impact. Judges have, therefore, felt relatively helpless, and reluctant to hold out promises that the law could not redeem.

The intractability of the problem in

large and medium cities has consequences also for smaller urban communities, in which demographic conditions might more readily permit some dispersal of racial groups through the school system. For it is one thing to tell district judges in the South, as the Warren Court did, that no single rule of thumb exists concerning methods of desegregation, and that different conditions might make different methods appropriate in various communities. It is one thing also, as the Court too seldom did, to withhold centralized national law, and allow private institutions or local governments to evolve diverse policies. Diversity of school policies exists now, pursuant to the play of state and local initiative. A number of communities are making their own efforts to achieve better racial balance in their schools. It is quite another thing, however, to issue, out of the same federal judiciary, one binding rule of constitutional law for Manhasset, New York, let us say (*de facto* segregation is unconstitutional and measures, such as school pairing and busing and transfer plans, must be taken to balance the races in the schools), and a different rule of constitutional law for New York City (*de facto* segregation is inevitable and hence not unconstitutional). . . .

Proposals answering to the revived desire that the school be less a creature of the state and its law, and more an extension of the self-directed home range from decentralization plans to tuition-grant schemes. Following a recommendation of the New York City Board of Education, the New York legislature in 1969 subdivided the city's school system into at least thirty community districts, with a student population as small as 20,000 each, though no smaller. . . . The legislation enacted in 1969 gives the local boards all too little direct and specific power over curriculum and teachers, and the sense of community may in these circumstances wither. If it is sustained, however, more power may be expected to flow to the local boards. . . .

Decentralization schemes like New York City's, which retain the public school as such, have already received strong support from virtually all segments of Negro opinion. Even in litigation, where this sort of thing is apt to manifest itself last, an impatience on the part of some Negro groups, although to be sure not all, with integration palliatives has begun to exhibit itself. Tuition plans, in combination with the continued existence of some public schools, or as an ultimate goal implying the abandonment of public schools, may also commend themselves to Negro groups, as they undoubtedly will to parochial-school parents. A body of law, flowing naturally out of *Brown* v. *Board of Education* broadly conceived, will bar the way, however, unless substantially modified or abandoned.

We noted earlier a series of school-closing cases in the South in which the act of closing the schools, always selective, was by the plainest and most unmistakable evidence part of a strategy for maintaining segregation. For this reason, the courts, including in the *Prince Edward County* case the Supreme Court, ordered the schools reopened. Tuition plans that were tied entirely to school closings of this ilk, and were meant to tide whites over in temporary quasi-public schools until the segregated situation could be restored in the regular ones, were also struck down.

After massive resistance to desegregation in any form was broken, however, a number of Southern states enacted tuition-grant statutes that could no longer be viewed quite so plainly as part of an effort to continue segregation in the public schools. The question now, formally, was of the reach of constitutional law, and of the nature and extent of private ordering to which the law of the Constitution is not applicable, and which is not subject to supervision and regulation by the federal courts. . . .

No doubt, schools and any other institutions mainly supported by tuition grants may and should still be held subject to the minimal rule of *Brown* v. *Board of Education,* which forbids state-enforced or state-sponsored segregation. An appreciable number will in fact be integrated, as many private schools are now. Yet assuredly many private schools, as also many decentralized public schools, would be *de facto* segregated, or nearly so.

We cannot, said the Court in *Brown* v. *Board of Education,* "turn the clock back to 1868 when the [Fourteenth] Amendment was adopted, or even to 1896 when *Plessy* v. *Ferguson* was written. We must consider public education in light of its full development and its present place in American life throughout the Nation." That development, we now know, was not full and not final at the time of *Brown,* and that place is changing. What the *Brown* opinion ultimately envisioned seems for the moment unattainable, and is becoming unwanted. Soon it may be impossible to "turn the clock back" to 1954, when *Brown* v. *Board of Education* was written. This is not to detract from the nobility of the Warren Court's aspiration in *Brown,* nor from the contribution to American life of the rule that the state may not coerce or enforce the separation of the races. But it is to say that *Brown* v. *Board of Education,* with emphasis on the education part of the title, may be headed for—dread word—irrelevance.

YALE KAMISAR (b. 1929), professor of constitutional law at the University of Michigan Law School, has been a strong supporter of active judicial protection of civil liberties and civil rights. He has written several books on criminal procedure and is co-author of a leading casebook on constitutional law. The selection below is taken from a preface he wrote to the recently published oral arguments before the Supreme Court in the *Brown* case. Kamisar finds the greatest impact of *Brown* in its symbolic quality, which affected both whites and blacks, especially on viewing the ugly face of resistance in some parts of the South. *Brown* thus set in motion the forces leading to a new black consciousness. Does it seem that Kamisar, like Bickel, has overstressed his case? Can it be fairly said, for instance, that the Black Upheaval was the result not of Court prodding but of Court failure?*

Yale Kamisar

An Optimistic View: Brown *and the Black Revolution*

Lord, we ain't what we oughta be,
we ain't what we wanna be,
we ain't what we gonna be but,
thank God, we ain't what we was.
—The Rev. Martin Luther King, Jr.
quoting an old southern preacher.

White southerners and Black men, as do *all* men, live by symbols. And in large measure the School Desegregation cases were so fiercely contested and then so bitterly resisted because school segregation is a special symbol. Indeed, to the southern Black this racist institution must have seemed the epitome of American hypocrisy. Had not Horace Mann called education "the great equalizer of the conditions of men?" Had not Justice Frankfurter called the public school "the symbol of our democracy and the most pervasive means for promoting our common destiny?" . . .

The Blacks understood, no less than did white southerners, that for the latter—or more accurately, for whites *everywhere*—to treat them as though they were outside the community of man it was

*Excerpts from pp. xiii–xxx from *Argument: The Complete Oral Argument Before the Supreme Court in Brown* v. *Board of Education of Topeka 1952–1955,* edited by Leon Friedman. Copyright © 1969 by Chelsea House Publishers. Reprinted by permission of Random House, Inc. Most footnotes omitted.

essential to nourish and preserve the stereotype of Blacks, the stereotype that—

> depicts Negroes as relatively unteachable, and therefore ignorant; as insensitive to the demands of abstract ideals, and therefore less troubled by discrimination than the white man; as motivated solely by appetite for the creature comforts, and therefore appeasable with access to fried fish, liquor and women; as devoid of moral fibre, and therefore predisposed to crime . . . [and] that segregation's significant function is not to deliver an insult but to preserve the group stereotype by minimizing contact between the races in situations where they would necessarily see and deal with each other as individuals, and by putting the official imprimatur on the proposition that Negroes and whites differ in a legally material way.

Similarly, Anthony Lewis has observed:

> That racial separation should carry more emotional weight in schools than elsewhere was understandable: Attendance was compulsory, and in school children of an impressionable age were exposed to a culture. Intermingling of the races could not help but affect their outlook. Putting it another way, any breakdown in school segregation necessarily endangered the perpetuation of the southern myth that the Negro is by nature culturally distinct and inferior. And there was the fear—surely felt deeply by many in the South, however others regarded it—that school integration was a step toward intermarriage.
>
> It was these reasons that led Hodding Carter, one of the most enlightened voices in Mississippi, to write a year before the School decision that a Supreme Court ruling against segregation would be "revolutionary" in character.

"Revolutionary in character?" Has it really turned out that way?

Up through the 1962–63 school year, less than 1 per cent of Black students attended school with whites in the eleven states of the old Confederacy. In the 1965–66 school year—in no small measure as a result of the Civil Rights Act of 1964 and guidelines promulgated by the United States Department of Health, Education and Welfare—the percentage increased to 6 per cent. . . . Although the rate of desegregation has accelerated almost everywhere in the South in recent years (the pace has been heartening in some states), the grim facts are that more Black students still attend all-Black schools in southern and border states than they did at the time of the first *Brown* decision—and this amounts to more than 75 per cent of all Black students in such states. Is this the stuff of "revolution"?

Even in the North, because of housing segregation, most Blacks, although legally eligible to attend white schools, are still in segregated ones. Indeed, in too many northern communities, because whites are moving away or sending their children to private or parochial schools, we are experiencing "resegregation." And most of the relatively few Black students who are no longer "separate" are not yet "equal" or meaningfully "integrated."

The statistical story is disappointing, but it is only a small part of the whole story. The consequences of *Brown* cannot begin to be measured by cold statistics. Nor, although the Supreme Court quickly applied (or extended) the principle of its 1954 ruling to other public facilities—such as public transportation, parks, and beaches, can its consequences be measured by the number of times it has been cited in other judicial opinions. Regardless of its practical, tangible, direct effects, and its judicial progeny, the symbolic quality of the decision was immeasurable. . . . It stimulated men everywhere—corporate executives, union officials, clergymen, hospital administrators, university executive officers and faculty members—to rethink and, sometimes at least, to reshape their policies. "Its educative and moral impact in areas other than public education and, in fact, its whole thrust toward equality and opportunity for all men has been of enormous importance." This impact and thrust, for example, contributed mightily to the enactment of the Civil Rights Acts of 1957, 1960, 1964, 1968, and the Voting Rights Act of 1965. . . . And it greatly accelerated, perhaps even precipitated, the "revolution" in constitutional-criminal procedure. For "it is hard to conceive of a Court that would accept the challenge of guaranteeing the rights of Negroes and other disadvantaged groups to equality before the law and at the same time do nothing to ameliorate the invidious discrimination between rich and poor which existed in the criminal process."

White America was never to be the same after *Brown*. Nor was Black America. As author Louis Lomax put it:

> It would be impossible for a white person to understand what happened within black breasts on that Monday. An ardent segregationist has called it "Black Monday." He was so right, but for reasons other than the ones he advances: That was the day we won; the day we took the white man's laws and won our case before an all-white Supreme Court with a Negro lawyer, Thurgood Marshall, as our chief counsel. And we were proud.

That the case generated a feeling of hope and momentum is evidenced by such Black responses to a national poll, years later, as: "It started the ball rolling": "the Supreme Court gave us heart to fight."[1]. . .

Southern conservatives understood perhaps better than northern liberals that revolution feeds on itself and that the time to stop one is at the beginning, not the end. But they couldn't. That is why *Brown* is a momentous decision.

Southern conservatives knew, too, that one Black success would lead to other Black demands. "They were undoubtedly wrong in thinking that they could hold the line by opposing all Negro demands, but the northern liberals were probably equally wrong in thinking that they could contain the Negro revolution by legal concessions."

I realize that revolutions do not begin at a particular point in time; that they are not made, but come, out of the past. Nor am I unaware that many factors were working for change in American race relations on the eve of *Brown*. "But revolutions require a spark, a catalyst. For the revolution in American race relations, this was the School Segregation case." Anthony Lewis said further:

> The struggle to carry out the Supreme Court's decision created a climate that encouraged the Negro to protest against segregation on buses, to demand coffee at a lunch counter, to stand in long, patient lines waiting to take a biased test for the right to vote. It was easy to say . . . that it would be more logical for Negroes in the South to concentrate on obtaining the ballot because political power would open the way to all other rights. But that was only true in the abstract. In the real world the right to vote was too remote an idea to arouse the Negro of the South from apathy and fear. It took the drama of school desegregation, and then of the protest movements, to make the possibility of freedom come alive; then Negroes began demanding *en masse* the ballot to which the law had said they were entitled. . . .

For southern Black families, two Black psychiatrists have recently told us, "School . . . was seen in a very special way. Beset on all sides by a cruel enemy, school was often primarily a refuge—a place of safety for those who were to be

[1] These were typical responses to a 1963 *Newsweek* national poll which found two-thirds of all Blacks crediting the Supreme Court for their biggest breakthroughs.

protected—and in a sense it was a case of women and children first." But after *Brown* little Black boys and girls left their refuge to face the cruel enemy.

The courage of these little pioneers of school desegregation inspired Blacks everywhere. And at a time when not a few northerners must have been growing a bit tired of it all—here as elsewhere people may go to great lengths to gratify reformers "in principle" only to find it rather tedious of them to insist on carrying principle to the point where it really bites—the ridicule, harassment and hatred of the white adults who confronted these Black children mobilized northern opinion in support of the Court's decision.

Few northerners would be misled any longer by "the entirely sincere protestations of many southerners that segregation is 'better' for the Negroes, is not intended to hurt them"; many would now understand "that what is meant is that it is better for the Negroes to accept a position of inferiority, at least for the indefinite future." On seeing the fury of the mobs and hearing "the ugly, spitting curse 'Nigger!'", the abstraction of racism was "concretized" on millions of television screens and the "moral bankruptcy" and "shame" of the thing finally grasped. The North was roused. And an aroused North meant an aroused Federal Government.

Many campaigns of the Black Revolution remain to be won—for example, de facto segregation and massive educational and economical issues. But on the fifteenth anniversary of *Brown* in large part thanks to those who did not spare us the gory details of "the southern way of life," the outcome of the campaign against legal, formal segregation of schools and other public facilities is no longer in doubt.

There remain, to be sure, pockets of resistance, some discouragingly large, many bitterly defended. Flushing them all out will take not a few years and in the process, no doubt, more hate will be spewed and more blood spilled. But now *this* campaign is only a mopping-up operation.

While an associate counsel for the NAACP, LEWIS M. STEEL (b. 1937) published an article in *The New York Times* on October 13, 1969, that occasioned a tremendous furor among liberal supporters of the Warren Court. Steel's charges that the Court still was and always had been a white man's court led to his abrupt dismissal by the executive secretary of the NAACP. (Steel is white, which makes this episode doubly ironic.) He is currently a member of a New York City law firm. Steel's article reviews the Court's major decisions affecting blacks since 1883 (he refers to most cases without naming them, and the student may wish to match his descriptions with titles for the cases as derived from the other readings), and concludes that the Court has always backtracked from full racial equality whenever the interests of whites were at stake. The question is obvious: Is Steel fair to the Court? Is his article mostly truth or mostly distortion?*

Lewis M. Steel

Still a White Man's Court

Historically, the Supreme Court has been the enemy of the American black man. During the 15 years in which Earl Warren has presided as Chief Justice, the Court has eliminated from the law books some of its more atrocious decisions. But never has it indicated that it is committed to a society based upon principles of absolute equality.

Popular belief has it that the Court deserves the major credit for awakening the nation to its civil rights responsibilities in 1954, when the justices decided that enforced segregation in our public schools violated constitutional precepts. With resolute firmness, according to both detractors and supporters, the Court has continued to strike down segregation and discrimination on every occasion. And, according to the traditional viewpoint, both the executive and legislative branches of our Government have lagged behind the Warren Court.

Because I believe, along with the National Advisory Commission on Civil Disorders, that "our nation is moving toward two societies, one black, one white—separate and unequal," I feel that all our institutions must be re-examined. A re-evaluation of the role of the United States Supreme Court discloses

*Lewis M. Steel, "Nine Men in Black Who Think White," *The New York Times Magazine,* October 13, 1968.

that it has struck down only the symbols of racism while condoning or overlooking the ingrained practices which have meant the survival of white supremacy in the United States, North and South. The Court has time and again taken the position that racial equality should be subordinated—or at least balanced against—white America's fear of rapid change, which would threaten its time-honored prerogatives. Only where racial barriers were overtly obnoxious—and, therefore, openly contradictory to the American creed of equality—has the Court deigned to move. Yet its decisions have allowed a confused, miseducated and prejudiced white public to believe that its black fellow citizens have been given their full rights.

To understand the Supreme Court's role in the civil rights movement and its peculiar obligation to insure equality for Negroes, it is imperative to understand the Court's role in establishing segregation in America. In the post-Civil War years, the Supreme Court led the nation away from the Reconstruction Congress's program for full citizenship for the freedmen. Congress passed five civil rights acts between 1866 and 1875. The 1875 act contained some strong public-accommodations sections that forbade racial discrimination in inns, public conveyances, theaters and other places of public amusement. When the act was first tested in the Supreme Court eight years later, the public-accommodations sections were struck down as unconstitutional; the opinion completely ignored the intent of Congress in passing the act and in proposing to the states the 13th and 14th Amendments. The Supreme Court thus opened the door for the passage of Jim Crow legislation.

Then, in 1896, the Court endorsed the establishment of a quasi-slave caste system by ruling that the states could require the segregation of public facilities as long as Negroes were provided equal accommodations. Three years later, the Court allowed Georgia to support a white high school while failing to provide secondary education for Negro children. This action destroyed even the myth of equality. Finally, in 1906, the High Court ruled that Congress had no constitutional authority to pass laws which would protect Negroes from harassment by whites solely on racial grounds.

Taken together, these cases meant that, in the Supreme Court's view, Congress could not protect Negroes from attack by their former masters and that state legislatures could pass laws which compelled a caste system.

Until 1954, the Supreme Court left its handiwork virtually alone. True, in the grandfather-clause and white-supremacy cases it disapproved of obvious measures to disfranchise Negroes completely, and in 1947 it prohibited the judicial enforcement of racially restrictive covenants attached to land deeds. But these decisions had no effect on the totally segregated society. Nor did they secure the vote to Negroes terrorized by white oppression. And, significantly, in 1950 the Court declined to review its own insidious creation, the separate-but-equal doctrine, when requested to do so in a case involving the right of a Negro student to attend the University of Texas Law School.

Long before the Court undertook any serious review of its constitutional doctrines in the field of race relations, other American institutions were re-evaluating their stands. During World War II and shortly thereafter, various agencies created machinery to make it appear that racial equality had become a part of our public policy. Thus, Presidential executive orders forbade racial discrimination by the recipients of Government contracts, the armed forces ordered the integration of military units and certain states enacted a variety of antidiscrimination laws. The reasons for these faint-hearted shifts in public policy have been discussed by the Advisory Commission and others. The war against Nazi Germany had raised the issue of racism and heightened the expectations of Negroes, who, because of labor shortages, were offered good jobs for the first time. Additionally, policy makers realized that the continuation of America's brand of apartheid could damage our standing with the newly emerging nations. Most important, black Americans came out of the war determined to fight for their rights at home.

Seen in the light of these pre-1954 shifts in attitude, the school-desegregation case did little more than bring the Court up to date. Until the 1954 decision, the gains won by Negroes were more in the nature of favors to be dispensed or withdrawn at the pleasure of the white overlords. Being gifts, not rights, these pre-1954 "reforms" stood as paper testaments only. Segregated Army units still fought in Korea; Negroes were still condemned to unequal job opportunities in defense plants and were openly segregated in the public schools of Northern states which had antisegregation laws.

In 1954, the Court was in a position to serve notice on the American people that equality was an absolute right of all citizens, that this right came before all other rights and that its further subversion could not be tolerated. By taking this stance, the Court could not only have gone a long way toward relieving its conscience but it could also have established itself as a true constitutional court, dedicated to an impartial search for just principles, irrespective of race.

Instead, the Court chose to act in the manner of the practical political reformer. Rather than ordering sweeping desegregation, it ordered another hearing. A year later, the Court ruled that the South did not have to desegregate its schools immediately, it merely had to do so "with all deliberate speed." Never in the history of the Supreme Court had the implementation of a constitutional right been so delayed or the creation of it put in such vague terms. The Court thereby made clear that it was a white court which would protect the interests of white America in the maintenance of stable institutions.

In essence, the Court considered the potential damage to white Americans resulting from the diminution of privilege as more critical than continued damage to the underprivileged. The Court found that public reasons—the offense to white sensibilities—existed to justify the delay in school desegregation. Worse still, it gave the primary responsibility for achieving educational equality to those who had established the segregated institutions.

This decision to delay integration and ignore racially discriminatory mechanisms was more shameful than the Court's 19th-century monuments to apartheid. For, by the mid-20th century, there was no basis on which the Court's nine educated men could justify a segregated society. Scientific racism had been discredited and America had been exposed to the full implications of racism in Nazi Germany.

Moreover, the United States had proclaimed itself the guarantor of freedom by taking up the sword against international Communism. From a judicial standpoint, crimes against humanity had been defined and punished at Nurem-

waw

berg. American justices had shown themselves to be capable of harshness when judging another people guilty of ghettoizing and destroying an ethnic group. Their failure to take an equally strong position when reviewing the sins of their own countrymen—whose institutions, according to the Court itself, damaged "the hearts and minds" of Negro children "in a way unlikely ever to be undone"—will long remain as a blot on the record of American jurisprudence.

Unfortunately, however, the Court's treatment of public-school desegregation was only the beginning of a pattern of conduct. Its handling of subsequent race cases indicates that it remains the Supreme Court of white America.

After its 1955 decision requiring "all deliberate speed," the Court did enter a series of decrees which slowly struck down segregation in public transportation and in public facilities and recreational areas. These decisions, however, were directed only at overt discriminatory practices in the Southern and border states.

In the field of education, the Court refused to review a series of conservative lower-court decisions which upheld what school officials described as accidental segregation in Gary, Ind.; Kansas City, Kan., and Cincinnati. As a result, the schools of the North have become segregated faster than Southern schools have been desegregated. Moreover, in the South and border states, Supreme Court reviews of lower-court decisions have been so timid that only 15 per cent of all Southern black children attend other than totally segregated schools. True, the Supreme Court ordered last May that discrimination be eliminated "root and branch" from school systems. But this decision, coming 14 years after *Brown* v. *Board of Education* in 1954, will yield small dividends unless the Court also agrees to tackle the question of *de facto* segregation. And nothing the Court has done to date indicates that this step is on the agenda.

The Court has also reflected the views of the white community in first protecting Negro protest marches, then removing its protection after significant changes had taken place in American attitudes. When Negroes and their white supporters began demonstrating, they were considered to be humble supplicants seeking succor from white America. Toward the middle of the nineteen-sixties, civil rights demonstrators, rather than playing a humble role, proclaimed that they would not be moved. Negroes had become assertive in a society which considered such behavior anathema, and repression became the order of the day. White America, without any basis in fact, decided that demonstrations and riots were synonymous.

The Court's change in attitude was foreshadowed in *Cox* v. *Louisiana* in 1965, in which it reversed the convictions of Negro demonstrators but warned that the right to protest could be limited. The new approach was not based on a fundamental difference between recent demonstrations and earlier ones; nothing had occurred which would indicate that civil rights advocates had abandoned their philosophy of peaceful protest. The new restrictions against demonstrations were first applied in *Adderley* v. *Florida* in 1966. The Court held that, although there was no violence, a peaceful protest outside a police station could be curtailed. The inconsistency between this and earlier cases can be explained only in terms of a judicial concession to white anxieties.

Significantly, the Court's new approach was reflected in decrees detrimental to the moderate civil rights organizations it originally protected. Thus, the Court, which had earlier intervened to save the National Association for the Advancement of Colored People in Alabama, allowed the Georgia state courts to threaten the group's existence by awarding a huge money judgment against it in a suit seeking damages for picketing. In failing to sustain the N.A.A.C.P., the Supreme Court allowed the state courts to apply completely arbitrary rules of law. Even in the darkest days of anti-labor judicial decrees, the unions were never dealt with more harshly.

As public opinion in opposition to civil rights demonstrations mounted, the Supreme Court's position further hardened. In 1967, it allowed an obviously unconstitutional Alabama state-court injunction to serve as a vehicle for the jailing of the Rev. Martin Luther King.

This spring, in an even more damaging decision, the Court ruled in *Cameron* v. *Johnson* that a Federal court was correct in refusing to interfere with the prosecution of Mississippi civil rights demonstrators accused of nothing more evil than maintaining an orderly picket line.

These decisional changes were achieved by an extremely simple expedient. The majority of the Supreme Court justices began to accept the protestations of good faith made by racist public officials, where only a few years earlier the majority had evinced a willingness to look beyond self-serving statements to ascertain the facts. Indeed, the Court has had dissenters who have vainly and loudly protested the majority's new anti-Negro attitude in the realization that such decisions mean a surrender to racists.

As the Court began to rule against Negroes seeking to reverse state convictions, it also decided that civil rights advocates could not seek relief from oppressive state prosecutions by removing their cases to the Federal courts; the justices were willing to assume the impartiality of courts which were strongholds of segregationists. By narrowing Federal jurisdiction, the Court achieved substantially the same effect as its predecessors did when they decided in the 19th century that laws intended to protect Negroes were unconstitutional.

Similarly, after developing rules that Negroes could not be excluded from juries, the Court negated much of its progress. In *Swain* v. *Alabama,* it upheld the right of Southern prosecutors to challenge and remove all Negroes while selecting a jury. The Court overlooked the fact that a Negro had never sat on a civil or criminal jury in the county in question and accepted at face value the prosecutor's declaration that he would allow Negroes to serve under certain circumstances.

Supporters of the Court's civil rights record can point only to the field of housing when seeking a pattern of pro-civil rights decisions, and the pattern fades when viewed critically. Since it struck down the judicial enforcement of restrictive covenants in land deeds in 1947, the Supreme Court has ruled favorably in California's Proposition 14 case and has upheld an 1866 law as a general prohibition against housing discrimination based upon race. The Proposition 14 case, decided in 1967, involved an amendment to the California Constitution which would have prohibited all state and local fair-housing laws and ordinances. The Court ruled this amendment unconstitutional. When, in the spring of this year, the Court upheld the 1866 law, it gave Negroes the right to sue individuals who refused to sell or rent property to them because of their race. Significantly, this ruling came after Congress had passed a fair-housing act. Once again, therefore, the Supreme Court, contrary to popular belief, was not the ground-breaker in racial reform. Moreover, neither the Proposition 14 case nor the endorsement of the 1866 law will significantly weaken ghetto walls. Most black Americans, having low incomes, will not be able to utilize these rulings, just as they were not able to profit much from the 1947 restrictive-covenant decision.

In 1967, the Supreme Court could have played a significant role in attacking ghetto housing. The case before it was *Green Street Association* v. *Daley*. The petitioners, Negro residents and a neighborhood association, complained that public officials in Chicago were using urban-renewal funds to create "a no-Negro buffer zone" around a white shopping center. In essence, the complaint alleged that the urban-renewal program, financed with public funds, was actually a program for Negro removal. The petitioners also said that the city was relocating Negroes only in ghetto areas, thus perpetuating housing segregation.

The complaint was dismissed by a Federal district court in Chicago and the decision affirmed by the circuit court. The Supreme Court, which could have ruled that these facts, if proved, would entitle the petitioners to relief under the 14th Amendment, declined to review the case. Again this year, when Negroes charged that highway construction in Nashville was being used to discriminate against the black community, the Supreme Court declined to review adverse lower-court decisions.

Favorable action in either of these cases would have done far more to aid the ordinary black man than all the other housing cases put together. For today, the effect of Government—local, state and Federal—on housing is far greater than that of individuals.

Those in the legal profession who defend the Court's record do so on the ground that the traditional relationship between the states and the Federal Government must be preserved. According to this theory, the liberties of all Americans are better preserved if the Federal Government is strictly limited in its right to oversee the affairs of the states; the restrictions, the theory says, prevent the creation of a monolithic centralized police state. According to these thinkers, an "activist" Supreme Court would be reliant on Federal power to enforce its writ in the states, thereby tipping an already precarious balance.

But what is this argument really worth? If basic civil rights can be denied on a systematic basis to any definable segment of the population, that segment is living in a police state. The justification of the Court's record presumes that constitutionally guaranteed freedoms should be analyzed from the point of view of the white American majority.

In effect, the argument is based on the premise that any threat, real or imagined, to the civil liberties of whites should be forestalled, even at the price of denying to black men the rights which may be hypothetically threatened by Federal intervention. For example, whites are afraid that *their* public school systems would be damaged by integration because black children attending segregated black schools perform at a lower academic level. Though the lower performance by Negroes has been brought about by the white community's treatment of Negroes as inferiors, integration has been delayed to save the white public schools at the further expense of black children.

Another argument in favor of judicial nonintervention is based upon the premise that in a democracy the people, through their legislatures, have the primary responsibility to redress grievances. This belief is also comforting only to the majority that completely controls the legislative process.

The fact is that the fabric of our country is threatened, not by theoretical considerations on the Federal-state relationship, but by the pervasive racism found by the Advisory Commission. "States' rights" is a phrase invented by the advocates of the status quo to stand as a philosophical bar to change. That politicians should grasp such a doctrine is to be expected; after all, politicians like to be able to tell their constituents that local problems are the result of outside interference. But Supreme Court justices should have no constituency; they are appointed for life to sit as judges over all the people.

In fields other than race relations, the Court has, to a much greater extent, acted without regard for popular opinion. Consider, for example, Supreme Court rulings in the fields of reapportionment, separation of church from state, obscenity, criminal law and the protection of Communists or others with unpopular political beliefs. In these areas, the Court has taken an active role in bringing about needed reforms. By and large, decisions in these fields have not been based upon a compromise between constitutional concepts and society's desire to preserve established institutions. . . .

The Court has not been so bold in race relations. Since the Civil War, it has allowed itself to be swayed by the prejudices and mores of whites and, more recently, by their fears that equality for Negroes would adversely affect them. In the 19th century, an activist Supreme Court helped the Southern states defeat Congress's plan to rid this country of all the remnants of slavery. In recent years, a cautious Supreme Court has waltzed in time to the music of the white majority—one step forward, one step backward and sidestep, sidestep.

ROBERT L. CARTER (b. 1917) has been adjunct professor of law at the New York University School of Law since 1966. Formerly general counsel of the NAACP, 1956–1968, he resigned along with his entire staff in protest at the dismissal of Lewis Steel (see preceding selection). The author of many articles dealing with various aspects of law, the Constitution, and the civil rights movement, Carter is presently a member of a New York City law firm. In this article, contributed in 1968 to a symposium on the Warren Court, Carter takes a moderate position between criticism and strong approval of the Warren Era in civil rights. The Court promised more than it could deliver, he holds, and thereby revealed the depth of the racial sickness in American society. But the Court did not retreat from its principles, even if unable fully to effectuate them.*

Robert L. Carter

Rhetoric and Reality: The Court's Middle Ground

When Chief Justice Warren assumed his post in October 1953, the underpinnings of the "separate but equal" concept had become unmoored beyond restoration. Full-scale argument on the validity of apartheid in public education was only weeks away, and the portent of change in the constitutional doctrine governing American race relations was unmistakable. Although the groundwork had been carefully prepared for the Chief Justice's announcement in *Brown* v. *Board of Education* that fundamental principles forbade racial segregation in the nation's public schools, the decision, when it was delivered on May 17, 1954, was more than a break with the past. In interpreting the fourteenth amendment as guaranteeing and securing to Negroes equality in substance rather than in mere form, the *Brown* decision was a revolutionary statement of race relations law.

Brown was the culmination of a trend, evident as early as *Missouri ex rel. Gaines* v. *Canada*, away from the arid and sophistical reading of the Civil War amendments marked by the legalisms of *Plessy* v. *Ferguson*. Instead, the Supreme Court in the first half of this century had begun to address itself to the task of formulating a pragmatic and realistic interpretation of what those amendments demanded in respect to the Negro's civil and political

*From *The Warren Court: A Critical Analysis*, edited by Richard H. Sayler, Barry B. Boyer, and Robert E. Gooding, Jr. Excerpts from pp. 46-56. Copyright © 1968 by the Michigan Law Review Association, © 1969 by Chelsea House Publishers. Reprinted by permission of Random House, Inc. Footnotes omitted.

status. "Sophisticated as well as simple-minded" modes of racial discrimination were understood to be within the Constitution's reach. The fourteenth amendment's guaranty of equal educational opportunity was said to be open-ended; it insured material equality; it encompassed intangibles not subject to objective measurement; and it forbade restrictions impairing and inhibiting a black student's ability to study and exchange views with other students.

With the decision in *Brown,* enforced racial segregation in education was put beyond the pale. More than that, the approach to which the Warren Court was fully committed required an examination and evaluation of any act, practice, or device which was undertaken with government sponsorship, in order to determine whether in purpose or effect black students were thereby denied their constitutional right to truly equal educational opportunity. Similarly, a like test seemed to be applicable in all other areas of governmental activity. *Brown* thus extended to its natural consequences could mean that the fetters binding the Negro were at last being struck, and that he would henceforth be able to stretch himself to his full potential.

Decision in the school desegregation cases began the Warren Court's long involvement in the development of race relations law. Subsequent opinions soon underscored the universality, permanence, and enduring nature of the newly announced constitutional doctrine. Segregation was struck down in public parks, in intrastate and interstate commerce, at public golf courses and other recreational facilities, in airports and interstate bus terminals, in libraries, and in the facilities of public buildings and courtrooms. Unlawful discrimination was found in the listing of candidates for public office by race on the ballot; in the Southern custom of addressing black witnesses by their first name; and in making marriage and sexual relations between blacks and whites a crime.

In its refusal to tolerate open attempts to evade or frustrate compliance with *Brown,* the Warren Court made clear that the new doctrine was a fixed and permanent aspect of its approach to constitutional adjudication in the race relations field. In addition, a broadened definition of state action, encompassing all situations in which the state was significantly involved in supporting or encouraging discrimination, extended the reach of the fourteenth amendment. The court ruled that a state is under no affirmative obligation to enact antidiscrimination legislation, and that when such laws are promulgated, they may be repealed; but the Court added the precautionary caveat that if in the process of repeal the state tips the political balance in favor of racial discrimination, it violates the fourteenth amendment.

The Court also sought to strengthen and further the desegregation process by protecting and undergirding the peaceful self-help activities of those individuals and groups seeking to eliminate segregation. The rationale for extending the constitutional guarantees of freedom of association and expression to membership in civil rights groups and their sponsorship of test litigation reveals the Warren Court at its best in adapting the Constitution's safeguards to real-life situations. Until the Civil Rights Act of 1964 empowered the federal government to use its resources in furthering desegregation, the only method available to secure compliance with *Brown* in the face of resistance was affirmative action by individuals or groups. The Supreme Court was sensitive to this problem, and when Alabama sought to still concerted group agitation and activity for desegregation by requiring public identification of all NAACP members in the state, the Court realized that such enforced disclosure would expose the members to coercion, intimidation, reprisals, and harassment. Recognizing that this would impair, if not destroy, concerted civil rights activity, the Court concluded that the constitutional guaranty of freedom of association embraced and included privacy in one's associational relationships, absent a countervailing state interest of compelling dimensions. Subsequently, in striking down state efforts to make group sponsorship of civil rights litigation unlawful, the Court correctly classified such court action as a protected form of political expression for the black community—and indeed for many years it was the only effective method of political expression available.

On the other hand, the Court's concern for keeping peaceful protest activity alive and its pragmatic approach to decision-making led to a rather bizarre development in the sit-in cases. While the Court was determined to support the efforts of college students to break the pattern of racial segregation in the South by organized sit-in activities, it was not prepared to extend *Shelly* v. *Kraemer* in order to prohibit state enforcement of private discrimination in places of public accommodation, or to break new ground by adopting some other approach to decision that would bar state use of its breach of the peace or trespass laws to defeat this kind of civil rights effort. Instead, it held to an ad hoc method of adjudication, rendering decisions good for one case and one case only. The Court came out on the right side in supporting and sustaining this form of peaceful protest, but its reasoning was strained and tortured. Its decisions kept the sit-in movement viable until enactment of the Civil Rights Act of 1964, which reduced racial discrimination in places of public accommodation to an issue of minor significance.

During the past fifteen years, the Supreme Court has undoubtedly concerned itself more with the affirmative development of substantive constitutional doctrine upholding equal rights than at any other time during its history. It has been criticized for its decisions and for its activism, but the criticism is misplaced. The Court in *Brown,* in requiring the elimination of enforced racial segregation as an essential prerequisite to equal education, did no more than the *Plessy* v. *Ferguson* Court had done in devising the separate-but-equal standard as an appropriate constitutional yardstick. Both Courts attempted to give what they saw as effective and meaningful import to the fourteenth amendment's guaranty of equal protection and, in so doing, both made national policy in the race relations field. *Plessy* paid homage to the equal rights verbiage of the fourteenth amendment while in fact legitimizing governmental subordination of blacks to whites. The rhetoric of *Brown,* on the other hand, sought to make the same grant of equality an ingredient of real life in the Negro community.

The problem is that while the Warren Court's rhetoric is broad and sweeping, its decisions have kept to a rather narrow path. It has in the main addressed itself solely to the task of outlawing formalized public discrimination—to the appearance rather than the substance of racism. The Court has not expanded or extended *Brown.* It has not dealt with the question of de facto school segregation—an issue which is as potentially explosive today as was formal segregation in 1954. Therefore, we do not know what equal education means in the context of Northern-style school segregation. Although the Court supported and protected the sit-in movement, it developed no cutting principles of law which would bar states from lending their weight, under the guise of enforcing criminal trespass laws, to the support of private discrimination practiced by restaurant or hotel owners.

White supremacy, with or without formalized public discrimination, is the pervasive evil—the unyielding and persistent deterrent to fulfillment of the aims of the thirteenth, fourteenth, and fifteenth amendments. However, while the Warren Court did not go as far as it could have in the development of the substantive constitutional doctrine which *Brown* augured, what it did accomplish is of great significance. The broad rhetoric is there to build upon in the future. As stated earlier, the Court has attempted to deal forthrightly with one aspect of the race relations question—formalized public discrimination. And here, except for the troublesome problem of school segregation, it has done quite well. Moreover, the Court's perseverance has helped considerably in revealing the true dimensions of the race problem which confronts the nation today. What is now crystal clear is that solution of this problem will involve state and federal efforts of the greatest magnitude. The elimination of formalized public discrimination will not suffice. . . .

Brown v. *Board of Education* fathered a social upheaval the extent and consequences of which cannot even now be measured with certainty. It marks a divide in American life. The holding that the segregation of blacks in the nation's public schools is a denial of the Constitution's command implies that all racial segregation in American public life is invalid—that all racial discrimination sponsored, supported, or encouraged by government is unconstitutional. As a result of this seminal decision, blacks had the right to use the main, not the separate, waiting room; to choose any seat in the bus; to relax in the public parks on the same terms as any other member of the community. This and more became their birthright under the Constitution.

Equal rights legislation could no longer be regarded as a gift benignly bestowed by an enlightened and liberal-minded electorate. Antidiscrimination laws were no longer great milestones; rather, they served merely as administrative machinery useful for accomplishing what the fundamental law required. While such machinery was, of course, vital and important, these statutes could now be critically assessed not in respect to the "good intentions" which led to their enactment, but rather in terms of the results achieved in alleviating the particular forms of discrimination they were supposed to regulate.

Thus, the psychological dimensions of America's race relations problem were completely recast. Blacks were no longer supplicants seeking, pleading, begging to be treated as full-fledged members of the human race; no longer were they appealing to morality, to conscience, to white America's better instincts. They were entitled to equal treatment as a right under the law; when such treatment was denied, they were being deprived—in fact robbed—of what was legally theirs. As a result, the Negro was propelled into a stance of insistent militancy. Now he was demanding—fighting to secure and possess what was rightfully his. The appeal to morality and to conscience still was valid, of course, but in a nation that was wont to describe itself as a society ruled by law, blacks had now perhaps the country's most formidable claim to fulfillment of their age-old dream of equal status—fulfillment of their desire to become full and equal participants in the mainstream of American life.

Brown's indirect consequences, therefore, have been awesome. It has completely altered the style, the spirit, and the stance of race relations. Yet the preexisting pattern of white superiority and black subordination remains unchanged; indeed, it is now revealed as a national rather than a regional phenomenon. Thus, *Brown* has promised more than it could give, and therefore has contributed to black alienation and bitterness, to a loss of confidence in white institutions, and to the growing racial polarization of our society. This cannot in any true sense be said to be the responsibility of the Warren Court. Few in the country, black or white, understood in 1954 that racial segregation was merely a symptom, not the disease; that the real sickness is that our society in all of its manifestations is geared to the maintenance of white superiority.

Having opened this Pandora's Box, the Court was left for a long time to handle the problem alone. It is to its credit that the Warren Court did not falter in its resolve or turn away from its commitment to cut away all government support for discrimination.

Widely known for his legal activism in behalf of civil rights as well as for his professional scholarship, ARTHUR KINOY (b. 1920) is professor of law at Rutgers School of Law. He is also a member of the Center for Constitutional Rights in New York City and a law partner with the famous trial attorney William Kunstler. In the spring of 1967 Kinoy published a long article in which he reexamined the *Civil Rights Cases* and *Plessy* v. *Ferguson* and concluded that the Court had improperly narrowed the Thirteenth Amendment as well as the Fourteenth. The Thirteenth Amendment had not only abolished formal slavery but had established a constitutional right of Negro freedom, which included the responsibility of the national government to uproot all the heritage of the slave system. Then in June 1968 came the case of *Jones* v. *Mayer,* in which the Court gave a stunning vindication to at least part of Kinoy's analysis. The article below was written by Kinoy immediately after that decision and heralds perhaps the future road the Court and the nation as a whole may travel to carry out at last the full promise of freedom for the black man.*

Arthur Kinoy

New Frontiers in the Struggle for Black Freedom

In an earlier article, *The Constitutional Right of Negro Freedom,*[1] the proposition was advanced that the reluctance of the Supreme Court, and indeed the entire legal profession, first to acknowledge and then to define the substantive rights created by the Civil War Amendments lies at the very heart of the most troublesome and disturbing questions which increasingly beset both the Court and the American Nation. In that article it was suggested that central to any solution of the complex legal problems engendered by the impact of a decade of black upsurges and upheavals upon tradition-encrusted concepts of law is a recognition that, in abolishing the institution of chattel slavery, the Nation had enacted a hundred years ago a new national constitutional right—the right of the black man in America to be free. This new national right of freedom for the black

[1] Kinoy, *The Constitutional Right of Negro Freedom,* 21 RUTGERS L. REV. 387 (1967).

*Arthur Kinoy, "The Constitutional Right of Negro Freedom Revisited: Some First Thoughts on *Jones* v. *Alfred H. Mayer Company,*" *Rutgers Law Review,* 22 (Spring 1968), 537–543. Most footnotes omitted.

race was no narrow manumission from bondage. It was a charter of "universal freedom" which carried with it the right of the race of freedmen to be henceforth free from the stamp of inferiority imposed by the badges and indicia of the institution of human slavery. This "charter of liberty"—this new national constitutional right of freedom for the black man—was designed to raise the legal status of the race from the slavery-imposed status of "inferior" beings to the status of free men and women, full and equal participants in the hitherto white political community which constituted the "people of the United States."

As the first article suggested, the constitutional implications of such an analysis of the nature of the new right enacted by the Wartime Amendments are sweeping. As a *nationally* created right, the constitutional right of black freedom under our constitutional scheme, must be affirmatively protected and preserved by national power. Upon each branch of the national government—legislative, executive, and judicial—would rest the duty to utilize the particular power vested by the Constitution in that branch to protect and enforce this sweeping national right of black men and women to be free in all areas of life from the stigma of inferiority embedded in the outlawed system of human slavery. Under the time honored principles of *McCulloch* v. *Maryland*, Congress would have the direct and plenary power and duty to protect and enforce in its full dimensions this right of black freedom. The executive would have the duty independently to employ the full panoply of its constitutional power to protect and enforce the nationally granted right. And the national courts, for their part, would have under the Constitution the duty to utilize the full creativity of federal judicial power to protect and enforce the nationally created right of black citizens to be forever free from the burdens of all concepts of racial inferiority which are perpetuated by the continued existence of badges and indicia of slavery.

On June 17, 1968, the last day of the October 1967 Term, the Court took the first, historic step since the turning point *Civil Rights Cases* in 1883 towards redefining the constitutional dimensions of the national right of Negro freedom. In *Jones* v. *Alfred H. Mayer Company*, an impressive majority of the Court joined Mr. Justice Stewart in reminding the nation that "'by its own unaided force and effect,' the Thirteenth Amendment 'abolished slavery and established universal freedom.'"

In *Jones* the Court upheld an effort by black citizens to invoke federal equity power to restrain racial discrimination by private individuals in the sale of real estate. The Court found statutory authority for this exercise of federal judicial power in one of the original Reconstruction statutes, the Civil Rights Act of 1866. Section one of this Act provided that "citizens, of every race and color . . . shall have the same right . . . to inherit, purchase, lease, sell, hold, and convey real and personal property . . . as is enjoyed by white citizens. . . ." In resting judicial action upon this statutory basis the Court was forced to face the ultimate question of the source for Congressional power to legislate in the area of purely private racially discriminatory action, whether or not sanctioned by state law. Accepting the challenge, the Court reached out and, for the first time since Reconstruction, found constitutional authority for congressional legislation in the area of Negro rights in the power created by the Thirteenth Amendment "'to pass *all laws necessary and proper for abolishing all badges and incidents of slavery in the United States.'"*[2]

I would suggest that the far reaching implications of this bold and calculated step cannot be underestimated. It is no accident that the Warren era opened with *Brown* v. *Board of Education* and closed with *Jones* v. *Alfred H. Mayer Company.* The pronouncements of the Court in *Jones* are not casual dicta. The words are written clearly and bluntly, and are meant, in the greatest tradition of the Court, to be read by the people. The decision could easily have gone off on any number of technical or refined points of constitutional exegesis. Federal action might have been sustained by stretching a little further the incredibly elastic "state action" dogma, as the Court has done so often in the past. Federal intervention could have been rejected through a process of convoluted balancing of "public interests" with the "right of private property," as the Court has too frequently engaged in recently. Decision might even have been avoided completely as mooted by the passage of the Fair Housing provisions of the Civil Rights Act of 1968, as the dissenting Justices argued with some justification.

But the Court took none of these readily available alternatives. In the words of a Southern member of the federal appellate judiciary, Judge John Minor Wisdom of the Fifth Circuit, who has been advocating this type of forthright stand for some time, the Court has at long last "grasp[ed] the nettle." For these reasons, I believe it is neither rash nor premature to open a discussion, even if tentative, which seeks to explore the implications of this extraordinary move on the part of the Court. Only by developing such a discussion will it be possible to begin to examine the far-reaching implications of the decision, including both possible limitations in its present formulations and the avenues it has suddenly and dramatically opened up for the creative expansion of the frontiers of the law of freedom and human rights.

It is impossible to overstate the potentially profound importance to the political and legal life of the Nation of the Court's beginning resurrection of the constitutional concept of the national right of Negro freedom from beneath the pile of ambiguities and distortions which have buried it since the betrayals of 1877. In the earlier article I explored certain of the serious problems which flowed from the failure of the original *Brown* v. *Board of Education* decisions to articulate squarely the nature of the rights involved in striking down a system of segregated education. The overt reluctance for over a decade of the executive and legislative branches to accept any primary responsibility for enforcing the sweeping conclusions of the Court in *Brown*—a reluctance which continues to persist despite official disclaimers to the contrary—is in a very real sense at the core of the frustration and anger which is welling up in the black ghettos and rural slums of the country. But this studied reluctance to assume primary and direct national responsibility for the enforcement of the rights of black citizens drew strength in large measure from the failure of the original opinions to develop any understanding that the right involved was in fact a *nationally* created right which constitutionally requires for its protection the invocation of direct and plenary *national* power. Such a concept of the right did not emerge in the original

[2] Jones v. Alfred H. Mayer Co. (citing Civil Rights Cases, emphasis by the *Jones* Court).

Brown opinions. This is because, for reasons to be explored, although the Court specifically overruled the *Plessy* v. *Ferguson* majority, it could not yet bring itself to face the awesome implications of the conceptual analysis of the first Justice Harlan in his *Plessy* dissent. . . . The first Justice Harlan put the question bluntly in words which ring with the same force as Mr. Justice Stewart's recent opinion in *Jones.* Enforced segregation of the races in any area of public life was, according to Harlan, a "badge of servitude wholly inconsistent with the civil freedom and the equality before the law established by the Constitution." It was a contemporary attempt to re-establish the concept of an "inferior race," the central ideological and legal foundation of the supposedly outlawed system of slavery. It was a device to keep the newly emancipated race of freedmen in a position equivalent to that of a "subject race," their former status under slavery. Within this context the right to be free from racial segregation in public education—as well as all other areas of public life—was a *national* right, essential to the establishment of the "universal civil freedom" decreed by the Wartime Amendments. It was a national right enacted by the Thirteenth Amendment and, as such, was an essential attribute of the citizenship created by the Fourteenth Amendment. Under the most hallowed principles of the federal union, the primary responsibility for enforcing such a right lay with the coordinate branches of the national government.

In 1954 the Court was obviously unwilling to develop such an analysis. One can only speculate upon the reasons. It could hardly have been that the Harlan concepts were not before the Justices; it is difficult to overrule *Plessy* without being keenly aware of the implications of the *Plessy* dissent. The reasons for the Court's unwillingness, I suggest, lie deep in our national psychology. In a certain sense we have all lived a lie for a hundred years. The Nation—the governing institutions and majority white population—has been unwilling to face the incredible reality of American history: the unspoken truth that a nation with such high pretensions to world leadership in science, culture, and democratic government could have tolerated for so long, in every section of the country, and in every aspect of its national existence, a way of life inherited from a system of society long condemned by the entire civilized world—the system of human chattel slavery. And yet this was and is the harsh and naked fact which conditions so much of contemporary American society. But this central historical fact—that the social system of slavery was never fully uprooted, and that its badges and indicia continued to brand the black man with the hallmark of slavery, the stamp of an "inferior race"—has been buried deep in our national consciousness. It is an unpleasant fact, an upsetting fact, one which is easier submerged than recognized, easier ignored than acknowledged. For almost a century, in every area of national thinking—political, social, cultural, and even the historical sciences—we have chosen to act blandly as if the abrasive truth were nonexistent.

And so, when the high Court now deliberately decides to brush aside the camouflaging rhetoric accumulated over the past decades, the vocabulary of "civil rights" and "equal protection of the laws," and bluntly characterize the "racial discrimination [which] herds men into ghettos" as "a relic of slavery," the potential significance of this formulation lies even beyond the enormous legal and constitutional implications which flow from this recognition of historical reality. I would venture to suggest that this profound understanding—that the vast and disturbing problems which are erupting from the black ghettos of America, urban and rural, are a direct consequence of white America's failure to uproot the vestiges of the barbaric system of human slavery—places those questions in the only perspective which will allow of their solution short of an expanding series of catastrophes and cataclysms which may well destroy the Nation. This understanding—that the gigantic problems of black poverty, discrimination, and second-class citizenship flow directly from the failure to enforce and implement the national commitment, one hundred years old, to abolish the slave system—creates a context for examining these questions which in turn settles all issues of national priority. . . . The elimination of the inferior status which characterizes the black citizens' position in housing, employment, and education, within such a context, can only be viewed as a national crisis question requiring the highest priority and the total commitment of every national resource. Any failure of the executive, legislative, or judicial branch to meet this crisis fully and adequately is not merely a failure to meet their normal governmental responsibilities; it is a flagrant brushing aside of their sworn duty to enforce constitutional obligations assumed a century ago.

It is in this sense that the pronouncements of the Court in *Jones* sweep far beyond the important legal and constitutional doctrines they augur. In response to what is perhaps the most fundamental role of the Court in our system of government—to be the ultimate teacher and reminder of those first axioms without which a democratic society cannot survive—the Court has sharply placed the most pressing problems of contemporary American society within a framework which should compel immediate national concern and national action. In this sense the *Jones* decision has the potential of being an historic step in the century old struggle for the fulfillment of the "universal human freedom" promised in the Wartime Amendments.

Plessy v. *Ferguson**

Error to the Supreme Court of the State of Lousiana.

No. 210. Argued April 13, 1896.— Decided May 18, 1896.

Mr. Justice Brown, after stating the case, delivered the opinion of the court.

This case turns upon the constitutionality of an act of the General Assembly of the State of Louisiana, passed in 1890 providing for separate railway carriages for the white and colored races. Acts 1890, No. 111, p. 152.

The first section of the statute enacts "that all railway companies carrying passengers in their coaches in this State, shall provide equal but separate accommodations for the white, and colored races, by providing two or more passenger coaches for each passenger train, or by dividing the passenger coaches by a partition so as to secure separate accommodations. *Provided,* That this section shall not be construed to apply to street railroads. No person or persons, shall be admitted to occupy seats in coaches, other than, the ones, assigned, to them on account of the race they belong to."

By the second section it was enacted "that the officers of such passenger trains shall have power and are hereby required to assign each passenger to the coach or compartment used for the race to which such passengers belongs; any passenger insisting on going into a coach or compartment to which by race he does not belong, shall be liable to a fine of twenty-five dollars, or in lieu thereof to imprisonment for a period of not more than twenty days in the parish prison, and any officer of any railroad insisting on assigning a passenger to a coach or compartment other than the one set aside for the race to which said passenger belongs, shall be liable to a fine of twenty-five dollars, or in lieu thereof to imprisonment for a period of not more than twenty days in

*Reprinted with minor abridgments.

the parish prison; and should any passenger refuse to occupy the coach or compartment to which he or she is assigned by the officer of such railway, said officer shall have power to refuse to carry such passenger on his train, and for such refusal neither he nor the railway company which he represents shall be liable for damages in any of the courts of this State."

The third section provides penalties for the refusal or neglect of the officers, directors, conductors and employés of railway companies to comply with the act, with a proviso that "nothing in this act shall be construed as applying to nurses attending children of the other race." The fourth section is immaterial.

The information filed in the criminal District Court charged in substance that Plessy, being a passenger between two stations within the State of Louisiana, was assigned by officers of the company to the coach used for the race to which he belonged, but he insisted upon going into a coach used by the race to which he did not belong. . . .

The constitutionality of this act is attacked upon the ground that it conflicts both with the Thirteenth Amendment of the Constitution, abolishing slavery, and the Fourteenth Amendment, which prohibits certain restrictive legislation on the part of the States.

1. That it does not conflict with the Thirteenth Amendment, which abolished slavery and involuntary servitude, except as a punishment for crime, is too clear for argument. Slavery implies involuntary servitude—a state of bondage; the ownership of mankind as a chattel, or at least the control of the labor and services of one man for the benefit of another, and the absence of a legal right to the disposal of his own person, property and services. This amendment was said in the *Slaughter-house cases,* 16 Wall. 36, to have been intended primarily to abolish slavery, as it had been previously known in this country, and that it equally forbade Mexican peonage or the Chinese coolie trade, when they amounted to slavery or involuntary servitude, and that the use of the word "servitude" was intended to prohibit the use of all forms of involuntary slavery, of whatever class or name. It was intimated, however, in that case that this amendment was regarded by the statesmen of that day as insufficient to protect the colored race from certain laws which had been enacted in the Southern States, imposing upon the colored race onerous disabilities and burdens, and curtailing their rights in the pursuit of life, liberty and property to such an extent that their freedom was of little value; and that the Fourteenth Amendment was devised to meet this exigency.

So, too, in the *Civil Rights cases,* 109 U.S. 3, 24, it was said that the act of a mere individual, the owner of an inn, a public conveyance or place of amusement, refusing accommodations to colored people, cannot be justly regarded as imposing any badge of slavery or servitude upon the applicant, but only as involving an ordinary civil injury, properly cognizable by the laws of the State, and presumably subject to redress by those laws until the contrary appears. "It would be running the slavery argument into the ground," said Mr. Justice Bradley, "to make it apply to every act of discrimination which a person may see fit to make as to the guests he will entertain, or as to the people he will take into his coach or cab or car, or admit to his concert or theatre, or deal with in other matters of intercourse or business."

A statute which implies merely a legal distinction between the white and colored races—a distinction which is founded in the color of the two races, and which must always exist so long as white men are distinguished from the other race by color—has no tendency to destroy the legal equality of the two races, or reëstablish a state of involuntary servitude. Indeed, we do not understand that the Thirteenth Amendment is strenously relied upon by the plaintiff in error in this connection.

2. By the Fourteenth Amendment, all persons born or naturalized in the United States, and subject to the jurisdiction thereof, are made citizens of the United States and of the State wherein they reside; and the States are forbidden from making or enforcing any law which shall abridge the privileges or immunities of citizens of the United States, or shall deprive any person of life, liberty or property without due process of law, or deny to any person within their jurisdiction the equal protection of the laws.

The proper construction of this amendment was first called to the attention of this court in the *Slaughter-house cases,* 16 Wall. 36, which involved, however, not a question of race, but one of exclusive privileges. The case did not call for any expression of opinion as to the exact rights it was intended to secure to the colored race, but it was said generally that its main purpose was to establish the citizenship of the negro; to give definitions of citizenship of the United States and of the States, and to protect from the hostile legislation of the States the privileges and immunities of citizens of the United States, as distinguished from those of citizens of the States.

The object of the amendment was undoubtedly to enforce the absolute equality of the two races before the law, but in the nature of things it could not have been intended to abolish distinctions based upon color, or to enforce social, as distinguished from political equality, or a commingling of the two races upon terms unsatisfactory to either. Laws permitting, and even requiring, their separation in places where they are liable to be brought into contact do not necessarily imply the inferiority of either race to the other, and have been generally, if not universally, recognized as within the competency of the state legislatures in the exercise of their police power. The most common instance of this is connected with the establishment of separate schools for white and colored children, which has been held to be a valid exercise of the legislative power even by courts of States where the political rights of the colored race have been longest and most earnestly enforced.

One of the earliest of these cases is that of *Roberts* v. *City of Boston,* 5 Cush. 198, in which the Supreme Judicial Court of Massachusetts held that the general school committee of Boston had power to make provision for the instruction of colored children in separate schools established exclusively for them, and to prohibit their attendance upon the other schools. "The great principle," said Chief Justice Shaw, p. 206, "advanced by the learned and eloquent advocate for the plaintiff," (Mr. Charles Sumner,) "is, that by the constitution and laws of Massachusetts, all persons without distinction of age or sex, birth or color, origin or condition, are equal before the law. . . . But, when this great principle comes to be applied to the actual and various conditions of persons in society, it will not warrant the assertion, that men and women are legally clothed with the same civil and political powers, and that children and adults are legally to have the same functions and be subject to the same treatment; but only that the rights of all, as they are settled and regulated by law, are equally entitled to the paternal consideration and protection of the law for their maintenance and security." It was held that the powers of the committee extended to the establishment of separate schools for children of different ages, sexes and colors, and that they might also establish special schools for poor and neglected children, who have become too old to attend the primary school, and yet have not acquired the rudiments of learning, to enable them to enter the ordinary schools. Similar laws have been enacted by Congress under its general power of legislation over the District of Columbia, Rev. Stat. D.C. §§ 281, 282, 283, 310, 319, as well as by the legislatures of many of the States, and have been generally, if not uniformly, sustained by the courts. . . .

In this connection, it is also suggested by the learned counsel for the plaintiff in error that the same argument that will justify the state legislature in requiring railways to provide separate accommodations for the two races will also authorize them to require separate cars to be provided for people whose hair is of a certain color, or who are aliens, or who belong to certain nationalities, or to enact laws requiring colored people to walk upon one side of the street, and white people upon the other, or requiring white men's houses to be painted white, and colored men's black, or their vehicles or business signs to be of different colors, upon the theory that one side of the street is as good as the other, or that a house or vehicle of one color is as good as one of another color. The reply to all this is that every exercise of the police power must be reasonable, and extend only to such laws as are enacted in good faith for the promotion for the public good, and not for the annoyance or oppression of a particular class. . . .

So far, then, as a conflict with the Fourteenth Amendment is concerned, the case reduces itself to the question whether the statute of Louisiana is a reasonable regulation, and with respect to this there must necessarily be a large discretion on the part of the legislature. In determining the question of reasonableness it is at liberty to act with reference to the established usages, customs and traditions of the people, and with a view to the promotion of their comfort, and the preservation of the public peace and good order. Gauged by this standard, we cannot say that a law which authorizes or even requires the separation of the two races in public conveyances is unreasonable, or more obnoxious to the Fourteenth Amendment than the acts of Congress requiring separate schools for colored children in the District of Columbia, the constitutionality of which does not seem to have been questioned, or the corresponding acts of state legislatures.

We consider the underlying fallacy of the plaintiff's argument to consist in the assumption that the enforced separation of the two races stamps the colored race with a badge of inferiority. If this be so, it is not by reason of anything found in the act, but solely because the colored race chooses to put that construction upon it. The argument necessarily assumes that if, as has been more than once the case, and is not unlikely to be so again, the colored race should become the dominant power in the state legislature, and should enact a law in precisely similar terms, it would thereby relegate the white race to an inferior position. We imagine that the white race, at least, would not acquiesce in this assumption. The argument also assumes that social prejudices may be overcome by legislation, and that equal rights cannot be secured to the negro except by an enforced commingling of the two races. We cannot accept this proposition. If the two races are to meet upon terms of social equality, it must be the result of natural affinities, a mutual appreciation of each other's merits and a voluntary consent of individuals. . . . Legislation is powerless to eradicate racial instincts or to abolish distinctions based upon physical differences, and the attempt to do so can only result in accentuating the difficulties of the present situation. If the civil and political rights of both races be equal one cannot be inferior to the other civilly or politically. If one race be inferior to the other socially, the Constitution of the United States cannot put them upon the same plane. . . .

The judgment of the court below is, therefore,

Affirmed.

MR. JUSTICE HARLAN dissenting.

By the Louisiana statute, the validity of which is here involved, all railway companies (other than street railroad companies) carrying passengers in that State are required to have separate but equal accommodations for white and colored persons, "by providing two or more passenger coaches for each passenger train, *or* by dividing the passenger coaches by a *partition* so as to secure separate accommodations." Under this statute, no colored person is permitted to occupy a seat in a coach assigned to white persons; nor any white person, to occupy a seat in a coach assigned to colored persons. The managers of the railroad are not allowed to exercise any discretion in the premises, but are required to assign each passenger to some coach or compartment set apart for the exclusive use of his race. If a passenger insists upon going into a coach or compartment not set apart for persons of his race, he is subject to be fined, or to be imprisoned in the parish jail. Penalties are prescribed for the refusal or neglect of the officers, directors, conductors, and employés of railroad companies to comply with the provisions of the act. . . .

Thus the State regulates the use of a public highway by citizens of the United States solely upon the basis of race.

However apparent the injustice of such legislation may be, we have only to consider whether it is consistent with the Constitution of the United States.

That a railroad is a public highway, and that the corporation which owns or operates it is in the exercise of public functions, is not, at this day, to be disputed. . . .

In respect of civil rights, common to all citizens, the Constitution of the United States does not, I think, permit any public authority to know the race of those entitled to be protected in the enjoyment of such rights. Every true man has pride of race, and under appropriate circumstances when the rights of others, his equals before the law, are not to be affected, it is his privilege to express such pride and to take such action based upon it as to him seems proper. But I deny that any legislative body or judicial tribunal may have regard to the race of citizens when the civil rights of those citizens are involved. Indeed, such legislation, as that here in question, is inconsistent not only with that equality of rights which pertains to citizenship, National and State, but with the personal liberty enjoyed by every one within the United States.

The Thirteenth Amendment does not permit the withholding or the deprivation of any right necessarily inhering in freedom. It not only struck down the institution of slavery as previously existing in the United States, but it prevents the imposition of any burdens or disabilities that constitute badges of slavery or servitude. It decreed universal civil freedom in this country. This court has so adjudged. But that amendment having been found inadequate to the protection of the rights of those who had been in slavery, it was followed by the Fourteenth Amendment, which added greatly to the dignity and glory of American citizenship, and to the security of personal liberty, by declaring that "all persons born or naturalized in the United States, and subject to the jurisdiction thereof, are citizens of the United States and of the State wherein they reside," and that "no State shall make or enforce any law which shall abridge the privileges or immunities of citizens of the United States; nor shall any State deprive any person of life, liberty or property without due process of law, nor deny to any person within its jurisdiction the equal protection of the laws." These two amendments, if enforced according to their true intent and meaning, will protect all the civil rights that pertain to freedom and citizenship. Finally, and to the end that no citizen should be denied, on account of his race, the privilege of participating in the political control of his country, it was declared by the Fifteenth Amendment that "the right of citizens of the United States to vote shall not be denied or abridged by the United States or by any State on account of race, color or previous condition of servitude."

These notable additions to the fundamental law were welcomed by the friends of liberty throughout the world. They removed the race line from our governmental systems. They had, as this court has said, a common purpose, namely, to secure "to a race recently emancipated, a race that through many generations have been held in slavery, all the civil rights that the superior race enjoy." They declared, in legal effect, this court has further said, "that the law in the States shall be the same for the black as for the white; that all persons, whether colored or white, shall stand equal before the laws of the States, and, in regard to the colored race, for whose protection the amendment was primarily designed, that no discrimination shall be made against them by law because of their color." . . .

It was said in argument that the statute of Louisiana does not discriminate against either race, but prescribes a rule applicable alike to white and colored citizens. But this argument does not meet the difficulty. Every one knows that the statute in question had its origin in the purpose, not so much to exclude white persons from railroad cars occupied by blacks, as to exclude colored people from coaches occupied by or assigned to white persons. Railroad corporations of Louisiana did not make discrimination among whites in the matter of accommodation for travellers. The thing to accomplish was, under the guise of giving equal accommodation for whites and blacks, to compel the latter to keep to themselves while travelling in railroad passenger coaches. No one would be so wanting in candor as to assert the contrary. The fundamental objection, therefore, to the statute is that it interferes with the personal freedom of citizens. . . . If a white man and a black man choose to occupy the same public conveyance on a public highway, it is their right to do so, and no government, proceeding alone on grounds of race, can prevent it without infringing the personal liberty of each.

It is one thing for railroad carriers to furnish, or to be required by law to furnish, equal accommodations for all whom they are under a legal duty to carry. It is quite another thing for government to forbid citizens of the white and black races from travelling in the same public conveyance, and to punish officers of railroad companies for permitting persons of the two races to occupy the same passenger coach. If a State can prescribe, as a rule of civil conduct, that whites and blacks shall not travel as passengers in the same railroad coach, why may it not so regulate the use of the streets of its cities and towns as to compel white citizens to keep on one side of a street and black citizens to keep on the other? Why may it not, upon like grounds, punish whites and blacks who ride together in street cars or in open vehicles on a public road or street? Why may it not require sheriffs to assign whites to one side of a court-room and blacks to the other? And why may it not also prohibit the commingling of the two races in the galleries of legislative halls or in public assemblages convened for the consideration of the political questions of the day? Further, if this statute of Louisiana is consistent with the personal liberty of citizens, why may not the State require the separation in railroad coaches of native and naturalized citizens of the United States, or of Protestants and Roman Catholics?

The answer given at the argument to these questions was that regulations of the kind they suggest would be unreasonable, and could not, therefore, stand before the law. Is it meant that the determination of questions of legislative power depends upon the inquiry whether the statute whose validity is questioned is, in the judgment of the courts, a reasonable one, taking all the circumstances into consideration? A statute may be unreasonable merely because a sound public policy forbade its enactment. But I do not understand that the courts have anything to do with the policy or expediency of legislation. . . .

The white race deems itself to be the dominant race in this country. And so it is, in prestige, in achievements, in education, in wealth and in power. So, I doubt not, it will continue to be for all time, if it remains true to its great heritage and holds fast to the principles of constitutional liberty. But in view of the Constitution, in the eye of the law, there is in this country no superior, dominant, ruling class of citizens. There is no caste here. Our Constitution is color-blind, and neither knows nor tolerates classes among citizens. In respect of civil rights, all citizens are equal before the law. The humblest is the peer of the most powerful. The law regards man as man, and takes no account of his surroundings or of his color when his civil rights as guaranteed by the supreme law of the land are involved. It is, therefore, to be regretted that this high tribunal, the final expositor of the fundamental law of the land, has reached the conclusion that it is competent for a State to regulate the enjoyment by citizens of their civil rights solely upon the basis of race.

In my opinion, the judgment this day rendered will, in time, prove to be quite as pernicious as the decision made by this tribunal in the *Dred Scott case*. It was adjudged in that case that the descendants of Africans who were imported into this country and sold as slaves were not included nor intended to be included under the word "citizens" in the Constitution, and could not claim any of the rights and privileges which that instrument provided for and secured to citizens of the United States. . . . The recent amendments of the Constitution, it was supposed, had eradicated these principles from our institutions. But it seems that we have yet, in some of the States, a dominant race—a superior class of citizens, which assumes to regulate the enjoyment of civil rights, common to all citizens, upon the basis of race. The present decision, it may well be apprehended, will not only stimulate aggressions, more or less brutal and irritating, upon the admitted rights of colored citizens, but will encourage the belief that it is possible, by means of state enactments, to defeat the beneficent purposes which the people of the United States had in view when they adopted the recent amendments of the Constitution. . . . Sixty millions of whites are in no danger from the presence here of eight millions of blacks. The destinies of the two races, in this country, are indissolubly linked together, and the interests of both require that the common government of all shall not permit the seeds of race hate to be planted under the sanction of law. What can more certainly arouse race hate, what more certainly create and perpetuate a feeling of distrust between these races, than state enactments, which, in fact, proceed on the ground that colored citizens are so inferior and degraded that they cannot be allowed to sit in public coaches occupied by white citizens? That, as all will admit, it the real meaning of such legislation as was enacted in Louisiana.

The sure guarantee of the peace and security of each race is the clear, distinct, unconditional recognition by our governments, National and State, of every right that inheres in civil freedom, and of the equality before the law of all citizens of the United States without regard to race. State enactments, regulating the enjoyment of civil rights, upon the basis of race, and cunningly devised to defeat legitimate results of the war, under the pretence of recognizing equality of rights, can have no other result than to render permanent peace impossible, and to keep alive a conflict of races, the continuance of which must do harm to all concerned. This question is not met by the sugges tion that social equality cannot exist between the white and black races in this country. That argument, if it can be properly regarded as one, is scarcely worthy of consideration; for social equality no more exists between two races when travelling in a passenger coach or a public highway than when members of the same races sit by each other in a street car or in the jury box, or stand or sit with each other in a political assembly, or when they use in common the streets of a city or town, or when they are in the same room for the purpose of having their names placed on the registry of voters, or when they approach the ballot-box in order to exercise the high privilege of voting. . . .

The arbitrary separation of citizens, on the basis of race, while they are on a public highway, is a badge of servitude wholly inconsistent with the civil freedom and the equality before the law established by the Constitution. It cannot be justified upon any legal grounds.

If evils will result from the commingling of the two races upon public highways established for the benefit of all, they will be infinitely less than those that will surely come from state legislation regulating the enjoyment of civil rights upon the basis of race. We boast of the freedom enjoyed by our people above all other peoples. But it is difficult to reconcile that boast with a state of the law which, practically, puts the brand of servitude and degradation upon a large class of our fellow-citizens, our equals before the law. The thin disguise of "equal" accommodations for passengers in railroad coaches will not mislead any one, nor atone for the wrong this day done. . . .

I do not deem it necessary to review the decisions of state courts to which reference was made in argument. Some, and the most important, of them are wholly inapplicable, because rendered prior to the adoption of the last amendments of the Constitution, when colored people had very few rights which the dominant race felt obliged to respect. Others were made at a time when public opinion, in many localities, was dominated by the institution of slavery; when it would not have been safe to do justice to the black man; and when, so far as the rights of blacks were concerned, race prejudice was, practically, the supreme law of the land. Those decisions cannot be guides in the era introduced by the recent amendments of the supreme law, which established universal civil freedom, gave citizenship to all born or naturalized in the United States and residing here, obliterated the race line from our systems of governments, National and State, and placed our free institutions upon the broad and sure foundation of the equality of all men before the law.

I am of opinion that the statute of Louisiana is inconsistent with the personal liberty of citizens, white and black, in that State, and hostile to both the spirit and letter of the Constitution of the United States. If laws of like character should be enacted in the several States of the Union, the effect would be in the highest degree mischievous. Slavery, as an institution tolerated by law would, it is true, have disappeared from our country, but there would remain a power in the States, by sinister legislation, to interfere with the full enjoyment of the blessings of freedom; to regulate civil rights, common to all citizens, upon the basis of race; and to place in a condition of legal inferiority a large body of American citizens, now constituting a part of the political community called the People of the United States, for whom, and by whom through representatives, our government is administered. Such a system is inconsistent with the guarantee given by the Constitution to each State of a republican form of government, and may be stricken down by Congressional action, or by the courts in the discharge of their solemn duty to maintain the supreme law of the land, anything in the constitution or laws of any State to the contrary notwithstanding.

For the reasons stated, I am constrained to withhold my assent from the opinion and judgment of the majority.

Brown et al. v. *Board of Education of Topeka et al.*

No. 1. Appeal from the United States District Court for the District of Kansas.*
Argued December 9, 1952.
—Reargued December 8, 1953.—
Decided May 17, 1954.

MR. CHIEF JUSTICE WARREN delivered the opinion of the Court.

These cases come to us from the States of Kansas, South Carolina, Virginia, and Delaware. They are premised on different facts and different local conditions, but a common legal question justifies their consideration together in this consolidated opinion.[1]

In each of the cases, minors of the Negro race, through their legal representatives, seek the aid of the courts in obtaining admission to the public schools of their community on a nonsegregated basis. In each instance, they had been denied admission to schools attended by white children under laws requiring or permitting segregation according to race. This

[1] In the Kansas case, *Brown* v. *Board of Education,* the plaintiffs are Negro children of elementary school age residing in Topeka. They brought this action in the United States District Court for the District of Kansas to enjoin enforcement of a Kansas statute which permits, but does not require, cities of more than 15,000 population to maintain separate school facilities for Negro and white students. Kan. Gen. Stat. § 72-1724 (1949). Pursuant to that authority, the Topeka Board of Education elected to estab-

*Together with No. 2, *Briggs et al.* v. *Elliott et al.,* on appeal from the United States District Court for the Eastern District of South Carolina, argued December 9–10, 1952, reargued December 7–8, 1953; No. 4, *Davis et al.* v. *County School Board of Prince Edward County, Virginia, et al.,* on appeal from the United States District Court for the Eastern District of Virginia, argued December 10, 1952, reargued December 7–8, 1953; and No. 10, *Gebhart et al.* v. *Belton et al.,* on certiorari to the Supreme Court of Delaware, argued December 11, 1952, reargued December 9, 1953.

segregation was alleged to deprive the plaintiffs of the equal protection of the laws under the Fourteenth Amendment. In each of the cases other than the Delaware case, a three-judge federal district court denied relief to the plaintiffs on the so-called "separate but equal" doctrine announced by this Court in *Plessy* v. *Ferguson,* 163 U.S. 537. Under that doctrine, equality of treatment is accorded when the races are provided substantially equal facilities, even though these facilities be separate. In the Delaware case, the Supreme Court of Delaware adhered to that doctrine, but ordered that the plaintiffs be admitted to the white schools because of their superiority to the Negro schools.

The plaintiffs contend that segregated public schools are not "equal" and cannot be made "equal," and that hence they are deprived of the equal protection of the laws. Because of the obvious importance of the question presented, the Court took jurisdiction.[2] Argument

---

lish segregated elementary schools. Other public schools in the community, however, are operated on a nonsegregated basis. The three-judge District Court, convened under 28 U.S.C. §§ 2281 and 2284, found that segregation in public education has a detrimental effect upon Negro children, but denied relief on the ground that the Negro and white schools were substantially equal with respect to buildings, transportation, curricula, and educational qualifications of teachers. 98 F. Supp. 797. The case is here on direct appeal under 28 U.S.C. § 1253.

In the South Carolina case, *Briggs* v. *Elliott,* the plaintiffs are Negro children of both elementary and high school age residing in Clarendon County. They brought this action in the United States District Court for the Eastern District of South Carolina to enjoin enforcement of provisions in the state constitution and statutory code which require the segregation of Negroes and whites in public schools. S.C. Const., Art. XI, § 7; S.C. Code § 5377 (1942). The three-judge District Court, convened under 28 U.S.C. §§ 2281 and 2284, denied the requested relief. The court found that the Negro schools were inferior to the white schools and ordered the defendants to begin immediately to equalize the facilities. But the court sustained the validity of the contested provisions and denied the plaintiffs admission to the white schools during the equalization program. 98 F. Supp. 529. This Court vacated the District Court's judgment and remanded the case for the purpose of obtaining the court's views on a report filed by the defendants concerning the progress made in the equalization program. 342 U.S. 350. On remand, the District Court found that substantial equality had been achieved except for buildings and that the defendants were proceeding to rectify this inequality as well. 103 F. Supp. 920. The case is again here on direct appeal under 28 U.S.C. § 1253.

In the Virginia case, *Davis* v. *County School Board,* the plaintiffs are Negro children of high school age residing in Prince Edward County. They brought this action in the United States District Court for the Eastern District of Virginia to enjoin enforcement of provisions in the state constitution and statutory code which require the segregation of Negroes and whites in public schools. Va. Const., § 140; Va. Code § 22–221 (1950). The three-judge District Court, convened under 28 U.S.C. §§ 2281 and 2284, denied the requested relief. The court found the Negro school inferior in physical plant, curricula, and transportation, and ordered the defendants forthwith to provide substantially equal curricula and transportation and to "proceed with all reasonable diligence and dispatch to remove" the inequality in physical plant. But, as in the South Carolina case, the court sustained the validity of the contested provisions and denied the plaintiffs admission to the white schools during the equalization program. 103 F. Supp. 337. The case is here on direct appeal under 28 U.S.C. § 1253.

In the Delaware case, *Gebhart* v. *Belton,* the plaintiffs are Negro children of both elementary and high school age residing in New Castle County. They brought this action in the Delaware Court of Chancery to enjoin enforcement of provisions in the state constitution and statutory code which require the segregation of Negroes and whites in public schools. Del. Const., Art. X, § 2; Del. Rev. Code § 2631 (1935). The Chancellor gave judgment for the plaintiffs and ordered their immediate admission to schools previously attended only by white children, on the ground that the Negro schools were inferior with respect to teacher training, pupil-teacher ratio, extracurricular activities, physical plant, and time and distance involved in travel. 87 A. 2d 862. The Chancellor also found that segregation itself results in an inferior education for Negro children (see note 10, *infra*), but did not rest his decision on that ground. *Id.,* at 865. The Chancellor's decree was affirmed by the Supreme Court of Delaware, which intimated, however, that the defendants might be able to obtain a modification of the decree after equalization of the Negro and white schools had been accomplished. 91 A. 2d 137, 152. The defendants, contending only that the Delaware courts had erred in ordering the immediate admission of the Negro plaintiffs to the white schools, applied to this Court for certiorari. The writ was granted, 344 U.S. 891. The plaintiffs, who were successful below, did not submit a cross-petition.

[2] 344 U.S. 1, 141, 891.

was heard in the 1952 Term, and reargument was heard this Term on certain questions propounded by the Court.[3]

Reargument was largely devoted to the circumstances surrounding the adoption of the Fourteenth Amendment in 1868. It covered exhaustively consideration of the Amendment in Congress, ratification by the states, then existing practices in racial segregation, and the views of proponents and opponents of the Amendment. This discussion and our own investigation convince us that, although these sources cast some light, it is not enough to resolve the problem with which we are faced. At best, they are inconclusive. The most avid proponents of the post-War Amendments undoubtedly intended them to remove all legal distinctions among "all persons born or naturalized in the United States." Their opponents, just as certainly, were antagonistic to both the letter and the spirit of the Amendments and wished them to have the most limited effect. What others in Congress and the state legislatures had in mind cannot be determined with any degree of certainty.

An additional reason for the inconclusive nature of the Amendment's history, with respect to segregated schools, is the status of public education at that time.[4] In the South, the movement toward free common schools, supported by general taxation, had not yet taken hold. Education of white children was largely in the hands of private groups. Education of Negroes was almost nonexistent, and practically all of the race were illiterate. In fact, any education of Negroes was forbidden by law in some states. Today, in contrast, many Negroes have achieved outstanding success in the arts and sciences as well as in the business and professional world. It is true that public school education at the time of the Amendment had advanced further in the North, but the effect of the Amendment on Northern States was generally ignored in the congressional debates. Even in the North, the conditions of public education did not approximate those existing today. The curriculum was usually rudimentary; ungraded schools were common in rural areas; the school term was but three months a year in many states; and compulsory school attendance was virtually unknown. As a consequence, it is not surprising that there should be so little in the history of the Fourteenth Amendment relating to its intended effect on public education.

In the first cases in this Court construing the Fourteenth Amendment, decided shortly after its adoption, the Court interpreted it as proscribing all state-imposed discriminations against the Negro race.[5] The doctrine of

---

[3] 345 U.S. 972. The Attorney General of the United States participated both Terms as *amicus curiae.*

[4] For a general study of the development of public education prior to the Amendment, see Butts and Cremin, A History of Education in American Culture (1953), Pts. I, II; Cubberley, Public Education in the United States (1934 ed.), cc. II–XII. School practices current at the time of the adoption of the Fourteenth Amendment are described in Butts and Cremin, *supra,* at 269–275; Cubberley, *supra,* at 288–339, 408–431; Knight, Public Education in the South (1922), cc. VIII, IX. See also H. Ex. Doc. No. 315, 41st Cong., 2d Sess. (1871). Although the demand for free public schools followed substantially the same pattern in both the North and the South, the development in the South did not begin to gain momentum until about 1850, some twenty years after that in the North. The reasons for the somewhat slower development in the South (*e.g.,* the rural character of the South and the different regional attitudes toward state assistance) are well explained in Cubberley, *supra,* at 408–423. In the country as a whole, but particularly in the South, the War virtually stopped all progress in public education. *Id.,* at 427–428. The low status of Negro education in all sections of the country, both before and immediately after the War, is described in Beale, A History of Freedom of Teaching in American Schools (1941), 112–132, 175–195. Compulsory school attendance laws were not generally adopted until after the ratification of the Fourteenth Amendment, and it was not until 1918 that such laws were in force in all the states. Cubberley, *supra,* at 563–565.

[5] *Slaughter-House Cases,* 16 Wall. 36, 67–72 (1873); *Strauder* v. *West Virginia,* 100 U.S. 303, 307–308 (1880):

"It ordains that no State shall deprive any person of life, liberty, or property, without due process of law, or deny to any person within its jurisdiction the equal protection of the laws. What is this but declaring that the law in the States shall be the same for the black as for the white; that all persons, whether colored or white, shall stand equal before the laws of the States, and, in regard to the colored race, for whose protection the amendment was primarily designed, that no discrimination shall be made "separate but equal" did not make its appearance in this Court until 1896 in the case of *Plessy* v. *Ferguson, supra,* involving not education but transportation.[6] American courts have since labored with the doctrine for over half a century. In this Court, there have been six cases involving the "separate but equal" doctrine in the field of public education.[7] In *Cumming* v. *County Board of Education,* 175 U.S. 528, and *Gong Lum* v. *Rice,* 275 U.S. 78, the validity of the doctrine itself was not challenged.[8] In more recent cases, all on the graduate school level, inequality was found in that specific benefits enjoyed by white students were denied to Negro students of the same educational qualifications. *Missouri ex rel. Gaines* v. *Canada,* 305 U.S. 337; *Sipuel* v. *Oklahoma,* 332 U.S. 631; *Sweatt* v. *Painter,* 339 U.S. 629; *McLaurin* v. *Oklahoma State Regents,* 339 U.S. 637. In none of these cases was it necessary to re-examine the doctrine to grant relief to the Negro plaintiff. And in *Sweatt* v. *Painter, supra,* the Court expressly reserved decision on the question whether *Plessy* v. *Ferguson* should be held inapplicable to public education.

In the instant cases, that question is directly presented. Here, unlike *Sweatt* v. *Painter,* there are findings below that the Negro and white schools involved have been equalized, or are being equalized, with respect to buildings, curricula, qualifications and salaries of teachers, and other "tangible" factors.[9] Our decision, therefore, cannot turn on merely a comparison of these tangible factors in the Negro and white schools involved in each of the cases. We must look instead to the effect of segregation itself on public education.

In approaching this problem, we cannot turn the clock back to 1868 when the Amendment was adopted, or even to 1896 when *Plessy* v. *Ferguson* was written. We must consider public education in the light of its full development and its present place in American life throughout the Nation. Only in this way can it be determined if segregation in public schools deprives these plaintiffs of the equal protection of the laws.

Today, education is perhaps the most important function of state and local governments. Compulsory school attendance laws and the great expenditures for education both demonstrate our recognition of the importance of education to our democratic society. It is required in the performance of our most basic public responsibilities, even service in the

---

against them by law because of their color? The words of the amendment, it is true, are prohibitory, but they contain a necessary implication of a positive immunity, or right, most valuable to the colored race,—the right to exemption from unfriendly legislation against them distinctively as colored,—exemption from legal discriminations, implying inferiority in civil society, lessening the security of their enjoyment of the rights which others enjoy, and discriminations which are steps towards reducing them to the condition of a subject race."

See also *Virginia* v. *Rives,* 100 U.S. 313, 318 (1880); *Ex parte Virginia,* 100 U.S. 339, 344–345 (1880).

[6] The doctrine apparently originated in *Roberts* v. *City of Boston,* 59 Mass. 198, 206 (1850), upholding school segregation against attack as being violative of a state constitutional guarantee of equality. Segregation in Boston public schools was eliminated in 1855. Mass. Acts 1855, c. 256. But elsewhere in the North segregation in public education has persisted in some communities until recent years. It is apparent that such segregation has long been a nationwide problem, not merely one of sectional concern.

[7] See also *Berea College* v. *Kentucky,* 211 U.S. 45 (1908).

[8] In the *Cumming* case, Negro taxpayers sought an injunction requiring the defendant school board to discontinue the operation of a high school for white children until the board resumed operation of a high school for Negro children. Similarly, in the *Gong Lum* case, the plaintiff, a child of Chinese descent, contended only that state authorities had misapplied the doctrine by classifying him with Negro children and requiring him to attend a Negro school.

[9] In the Kansas case, the court below found substantial equality as to all such factors. 98 F. Supp. 797, 798. In the South Carolina case, the court below found that the defendants were proceeding "promptly and in good faith to comply with the court's decree." 103 F. Supp. 920, 921. In the Virginia case, the court below noted that the equalization program was already "afoot and progressing" (103 F. Supp. 337, 341); since then, we have been advised, in the Virginia Attorney General's brief on reargument, that the program has now been completed. In the Delaware case, the court below similarly noted that the state's equalization program was well under way. 91 A. 2d 137, 149.

armed forces. It is the very foundation of good citizenship. Today it is a principal instrument in awakening the child to cultural values, in preparing him for later professional training, and in helping him to adjust normally to his environment. In these days, it is doubtful that any child may reasonably be expected to succeed in life if he is denied the opportunity of an education. Such an opportunity, where the state has undertaken to provide it, is a right which must be made available to all on equal terms.

We come then to the question presented: Does segregation of children in public schools solely on the basis of race, even though the physical facilities and other "tangible" factors may be equal, deprive the children of the minority group of equal educational opportunities? We believe that it does.

In *Sweatt* v. *Painter, supra,* in finding that a segregated law school for Negroes could not provide them equal educational opportunities, this Court relied in large part on "those qualities which are incapable of objective measurement but which make for greatness in a law school." In *McLaurin* v. *Oklahoma State Regents, supra,* the Court, in requiring that a Negro admitted to a white graduate school be treated like all other students, again resorted to intangible considerations: ". . . his ability to study, to engage in discussions and exchange views with other students, and, in general, to learn his profession." Such considerations apply with added force to children in grade and high schools. To separate them from others of similar age and qualifications solely because of their race generates a feeling of inferiority as to their status in the community that may affect their hearts and minds in a way unlikely ever to be undone. The effect of this separation on their educational opportunities was well stated by a finding in the Kansas case by a court which nevertheless felt compelled to rule against the Negro plaintiffs:

> "Segregation of white and colored children in public schools has a detrimental effect upon the colored children. The impact is greater when it has the sanction of the law; for the policy of separating the races is usually interpreted as denoting the inferiority of the negro group. A sense of inferiority affects the motivation of a child to learn. Segregation with the sanction of law, therefore, has a tendency to [retard] the educational and mental development of negro children and to deprive them of some of the benefits they would receive in a racial[ly] integrated school system."[10]

Whatever may have been the extent of psychological knowledge at the time of *Plessy* v. *Ferguson,* this finding is amply supported by modern authority.[11] Any language in *Plessy* v. *Ferguson* contrary to this finding is rejected.

We conclude that in the field of public education the doctrine of "separate but equal" has no place. Separate educational facilities are inherently unequal. Therefore, we hold that the plaintiffs and others similarly situated for whom the actions have been brought are, by reason of the segregation complained of, deprived of the equal protection of the laws guaranteed by the Fourteenth Amendment. This disposition makes unnecessary any discussion whether such segregation also violates the Due Process Clause of the Fourteenth Amendment.[12]

---

[10] A similar finding was made in the Delaware case: "I conclude from the testimony that in our Delaware society, State-imposed segregation in education itself results in the Negro children, as a class, receiving educational opportunities which are substantially inferior to those available to white children otherwise similarly situated." 87 A. 2d 862, 865.

[11] K. B. Clark, Effect of Prejudice and Discrimination on Personality Development (Midcentury White House Conference on Children and Youth, 1950); Witmer and Kotinsky, Personality in the Making (1952), c. VI; Deutscher and Chein, The Psychological Effects of Enforced Segregation: A Survey of Social Science Opinion, 26 J. Psychol. 259 (1948); Chein, What are the Psychological Effects of Segregation Under Conditions of Equal Facilities?, 3 Int. J. Opinion and Attitude Res. 229 (1949); Brameld, Educational Costs, in Discrimination and National Welfare (MacIver, ed., 1949), 44–48; Frazier, The Negro in the United States (1949), 674–681. And see generally Myrdal, An American Dilemma (1944).

[12] See *Bolling* v. *Sharpe, post,* p. 497, concerning the Due Process Clause of the Fifth Amendment.

Because these are class actions, because of the wide applicability of this decision, and because of the great variety of local conditions, the formulation of decrees in these cases presents problems of considerable complexity. On reargument, the consideration of appropriate relief was necessarily subordinated to the primary question—the constitutionality of segregation in public education. We have now announced that such segregation is a denial of the equal protection of the laws. In order that we may have the full assistance of the parties in formulating decrees, the cases will be restored to the docket, and the parties are requested to present further argument on Questions 4 and 5 previously propounded by the Court for the reargument this Term.[13] The Attorney General of the United States is again invited to participate. The Attorneys General of the states requiring or permitting segregation in public education will also be permitted to appear as *amici curiae* upon request to do so by September 15, 1954, and submission of briefs by October 1, 1954.[14]

It is so ordered.

---

[13] "4. Assuming it is decided that segregation in public schools violates the Fourteenth Amendment

"*(a)* would a decree necessarily follow providing that, within the limits set by normal geographic school districting, Negro children should forthwith be admitted to schools of their choice, or

"*(b)* may this Court, in the exercise of its equity powers, permit an effective gradual adjustment to be brought about from existing segregated systems to a system not based on color distinctions?

"5. On the assumption on which questions 4 *(a)* and *(b)* are based, and assuming further that this Court will exercise its equity powers to the end described in question 4 *(b)*,

"*(a)* should this Court formulate detailed decrees in these cases;

"*(b)* if so, what specific issues should the decrees reach;

"*(c)* should this Court appoint a special master to hear evidence with a view to recommending specific terms for such decrees;

"*(d)* should this Court remand to the courts of first instance with directions to frame decrees in these cases, and if so what general directions should the decrees of this Court include and what procedures should the courts of first instance follow in arriving at the specific terms of more detailed decrees?"

[14] See Rule 42, Revised Rules of this Court (effective July 1, 1954).

Table of Cases

Adderley v. *Florida*, 385 U.S. 39 (1966)
Alexander v. *Holmes*, 396 U.S. 19 (1969)

Bell v. *Maryland*, 378 U.S. 226 (1964)
Berea College v. *Kentucky*, 211 U.S. 45 (1908)
Bolling v. *Sharpe*, 347 U.S. 497 (1954)
Bradley v. *School Board*, 382 U.S. 103 (1965)
Brown v. *Board of Education*, 374 U.S. 483 (1954)
Brown v. *Board of Education* (*Brown II*), 394 U.S. 294 (1955)

Cameron v. *Johnson*, 390 U.S. 611 (1968)
Civil Rights Cases, 109 U.S. 3 (1883)
Cooper v. *Aaron*, 358 U.S. 1 (1958)
Cox v. *Louisiana*, 379 U.S. 536 (1965)
Cumming v. *Board of Education*, 175 U.S. 528 (1899)

Dred Scott v. *Sanford*, 60 U.S. 393 (1857)

Edwards v. *South Carolina*, 372 U.S. 229 (1963)
Ex parte Virginia, 100 U.S. 339 (1880)

Flemming v. *South Carolina Electric and Gas Company*, 351 U.S. 901 (1955)

Gayle v. *Browder*, 352 U.S. 903 (1956)
Gilliam v. *School Board*, 382 U.S. 103 (1965)
Gong Lum v. *Rice*, 275 U.S. 78 (1926)
Green v. *County School Board*, 391 U.S. 430 (1968)
Green Street Association v. *Daley*, 387 U.S. 932 (1967)
Griffin v. *County School Board*, 377 U.S. 232 (1964)

Hamm v. *City of Rock Hill*, 379 U.S. 306 (1964)
Henderson v. *United States*, 339 U.S. 816 (1950)
Holmes v. *City of Atlanta*, 350 U.S. 879 (1954)

Jones v. *Alfred H. Mayer Company*, 392 U.S. 409 (1968)

Louisville, N.O. & T. Ry. v. *Mississippi*, 133 U.S. 587 (1890)
Lupper v. *Arkansas*, 379 U.S. 306 (1964)

McCulloch v. *Maryland*, 17 U.S. 316 (1819)
McLaurin v. *Greenville*, 385 U.S. 1011 (1967)
McLaurin v. *Oklahoma State Regents*, 339 U.S. 637 (1950)
Mayor and City Council of Baltimore City v. *Dawson*, 350 U.S. 877 (1955)
Missouri ex rel. Gaines v. *Canada*, 305 U.S. 337 (1938)
Mitchell v. *United States*, 313 U.S. 80 (1941)
Monroe v. *Board of Commissioners*, 391 U.S. 450 (1968)
Morgan v. *Virginia*, 328 U.S. 373 (1945)

NAACP v. *Overstreet*, 384 U.S. 118 (1966)

Plessy v. *Ferguson*, 163 U.S. 537 (1896)

Raney v. *Board of Education*, 391 U.S. 443 (1968)
Roberts v. *City of Boston*, 59 Mass. 198 (1849)
Rogers v. *Paul*, 382 U.S. 198 (1965)

Shelly v. *Kraemer*, 334 U.S. 1 (1948)
Sipuel v. *Board of Regents*, 332 U.S. 631 (1948)
Slaughter-House Cases, 83 U.S. 36 (1873)
Strauder v. *West Virginia*, 100 U.S. 303 (1880)
Swain v. *Alabama*, 380 U.S. 202 (1965)
Swann v. *Charlotte-Mecklenburg Board of Education*, 402 U.S. 1 (1971)
Sweatt v. *Painter*, 339 U.S. 629 (1950)

United States v. *Cruikshank*, 92 U.S. 542 (1876)
United States v. *Harris*, 106 U.S. 629 (1883)
United States v. *Reese*, 92 U.S. 214 (1876)

Walker v. *City of Birmingham*, 388 U.S. 307 (1967)

Guide to Further Reading

The story of the Supreme Court and the black American since Emancipation has produced a wealth of fine, scholarly literature, but most of it by lawyer-participants and law professors. (Fortunately, lawyers often write with clarity and imagination, contrary to popular conceptions.) Professional historians shy away (unnecessarily) from writing analytically on the Supreme Court. In addition, like most Americans, until recently the historical profession gave little attention to the plight of the Negro after Reconstruction. He was the forgotten man of American "progressive" historiography.

In respect to the political and social background of the Negro's struggle, historians have made indispensable contributions, especially for the earlier period. C. Vann Woodward's *Reunion and Reaction: The Compromise of 1877 and the End of Reconstruction* (Boston, 1951) brilliantly analyzes the Compromise of 1877, which symbolized the coming of national reconciliation, with the understanding that the federal government would leave racial matters in southern hands. His more extensive *Origins of the New South, 1877–1913* (Baton Rouge, 1951) explores the southern scene in depth and variety. Woodward's most directly relevant book is his well-known *The Strange Career of Jim Crow* (New York, 1955, 1966), which argues persuasively that compulsory segregation was not an inevitable outcome of the end of Reconstruction, but rather the product of specific social and political forces converging in the early 1890s. For post-1877 politics at the national level as they affected the Negro, see Stanley P. Hirshson, *Farewell to the Bloody Shirt: Northern Republicans and the Southern Negro, 1877–1893* (Bloomington, Ind., 1962); and Rayford W. Logan, *The Betrayal of the Negro: From Rutherford B. Hayes to Woodrow Wilson* (New York, 1954, 1965).

For background on the "middle period" leading up to *Brown* v. *Board of Education*, the most significant works on the Negro and his time are two impressive sociological studies: Gunnar Myrdal's monumental *An American Dilemma* (New York, 1944, 1963); and E. Franklin Frazier, *The Negro in the United States* (New York, 1949, 1957). Both books, penetrating beneath the facade of "separate but equal" and revealing the suppressed contradictions of American life, were cited by Chief Justice Warren. Other good readings for this period are Alan P. Grimes, *Equality in America* (New York, 1964), chap. 2; and C. Vann Woodward, *The Burden of Southern History* (Baton Rouge, 1960), somewhat overrated but worthwhile.

On the Black Upheaval that forms the context of the post-*Brown* era, Louis E. Lomax, *The Negro Revolt* (New York, 1962), is a good beginning to a vast literature. Also illuminating are Anthony Lewis, *Portrait of a Decade: The Second American Revolution* (New York, 1964), based on *New York Times* news stories; Benjamin Muse, *Ten Years of Prelude: The Story of Integration Since the Supreme Court's 1954 Decision* (New York, 1964); Leon Friedman, ed., *Southern Justice* (New York, 1965), on the mockery of justice which confronted civil rights workers at every level of the southern judicial system; and the highly controversial *Report of the National Advisory Commission on Civil Disorders* (Washington, 1968), comparable for the recent period to the Myrdal and Frazier studies for the 1940s.

Focusing on civil rights history directly, a few books present a full chronological survey. Robert J. Harris, *The Quest for Equality: The Constitution, Congress and the Supreme Court* (Baton Rouge, 1960), a selection from which is included within, emphasizes the Equal Protection Clause from its philosophical roots through the *Brown* case. Loren Miller, *The Petitioners: The Story of the Supreme Court of the United States and the Negro* (New York, 1966), also excerpted within, narrates with extraordinary detail and human interest the course of Court decisions affecting blacks since the *Dred Scott* case; Miller's love for his black brothers *and* the Court often leads him into difficulty, but his history is an honest one throughout. Mary F. Berry, *Black Resistance / White Law: A History of Constitutional Racism in America* (New York, 1971), is a well-documented indictment of the Executive branch in particular for its constitutionally rationalized inaction *or* violence in support of white domination of black people. Two very useful and extensive documentaries are Albert P. Blaustein and Robert L. Zangrando, eds., *Civil Rights and the American Negro* (New York, 1968); and Richard Bardolph, ed., *The Civil Rights Record: Black Americans and the Law, 1849–1970* (New York, 1970). For a good review article on voting rights history, see Brainerd Dyer, "One Hundred Years of Negro Suffrage," *Pacific Historical Review,* 37 (February 1968), 1–20.

Concerning specific chronological periods, the origins of the Fourteenth Amendment have been reexamined in the 1950s and 1960s, with results confirming the solid earlier study of H. E. Flack, *Adoption of the Fourteenth Amendment* (Baltimore, 1908), which emphasizes nationalism and a broad interpretation. See Jacobus Ten Broek, *The Anti-Slavery Origins of the Fourteenth Amendment* (Berkeley, 1951); Howard J. Graham's jewel-like, "Our 'Declaratory' Fourteenth Amendment," *Stanford Law Review,* 7 (December 1954), 3–39; W. R. Brock, *An American Crisis: Congress and Reconstruction, 1865–1877* (New York, 1963). On intentions toward banning segregation, compare Alexander M. Bickel's restrictive view, "The Original Understanding and the Segregation Decision," *Harvard Law Review,* 69 (November 1955), 1–65, with Alfred H. Kelly's more expansive, "The Fourteenth Amendment Reconsidered: The Segregation Question," *Michigan Law Review,* 54 (June 1956), 1049–1086.

The Supreme Court's post-Reconstruction stance can be further examined in Charles W. Collins, "The Fourteenth Amendment and the Negro Race Problem," *American Law Review,* 45 (November–December 1911), 830–856, approving the Court's decisions; Edmond F. Waite, "The Negro in the Supreme Court," *Minnesota Law Review,* 30 (March 1946), 219–304, an elaborate review of cases; Barton J. Bernstein, "Plessy v. Ferguson: Conservative Sociological Jurisprudence," *Journal of Negro History,* 7 (July 1963), 196–205, which emphasizes the social assumptions of Justice Brown; Howard J. Graham, "The Waite Court and the Fourteenth Amendment," *Vanderbilt Law Review,* 17 (March 1964), 525–547, an excellent review-article of Magrath's biography of Chief Justice Waite (see third selection within); Otto H. Olsen, *The Thin Disguise: Plessy* v. *Ferguson: A Documentary Presentation* (New York, 1967), which prints the appellant's briefs as well as newspaper commentary on the decision; and Arthur Kinoy's powerful "The Constitutional Right of Negro Freedom," *Rutgers Law Review,* 21 (Spring 1967), 387–441, underscoring the continued relevance of Justice Harlan's great dissents. A fascinating contemporary critique of the Court's decisions was published anonymously in 1889 under the title *Justice and Jurisprudence* (reprinted by Greenwood Publishing Co., New York, 1969).

On the long, bleak stretch between *Plessy* and the 1940s, some light is cast by William B. Hixson, Jr., "Moorfield Storey and the Struggle for Equality," *Journal of American History,* 55 (December 1968), 533–554, the story of the pioneer NAACP cases before the Supreme Court. On the *Brown* decision, for additional *académie*-based arguments, see Charles S. Hyneman, *The Supreme Court on Trial* (New York, 1963), a political scientist's swinging indictment of the Court, which is accused of improper forcing of vast social change; and the defense by law professor Morris D. Forkosch, "The Desegregation Opinion Revisited: Legal or Sociological?", *Vanderbilt Law Review,* 21 (December 1967), 47–76, which compares, favorably to the Warren Court, the judicial function in *Plessy* and *Brown*.

The right-wing attack on *Brown,* which gained momentum after publication of the Byrnes article calling for a curb on the Court (see within), was productive, in some quarters, of an extraordinarily extravagant literature. Often the assault on the Court went far beyond

Brown to derogate the Warren justices and all their works. The most sophisticated of the genre is L. Brent Bozell's *The Warren Revolution* (New York, 1966), which argues that the Court sought to constitutionalize its own brand of consensus and thus abused judicial power. More rhetorical is the sweeping condemnation by Rosalie M. Gordon, *Nine Men Against America* (New York, 1958), complete with biographical innuendos of leftist associations for almost all the justices. This epitome of the "radical right" sees *Brown* as opening the way for centralized control of the schools, necessary to facilitate a "communist-socialist" take-over. For an unmitigated racist emphasis, see "revisionist" historian Charles Callan Tansill's address, "How Long Will Southern Legislatures Continue to Acquiesce in the Alleged Decision of the Supreme Court on May 17, 1954?", *Alabama Lawyer,* 23 (October 1962), 364–386. A variety of other right-wing criticisms of the Warren Court, and of *Brown* v. *Board of Education* in particular, will be found in Clifford M. Lytle, *The Warren Court: Its Critics* (Tucson, 1968).

Readers who wish to pursue the issue of the social science testimony in *Brown* may consult Kenneth B. Clark, "The Desegregation Cases: Criticism of the Social Scientists' Role," *Villanova Law Review,* 5 (Winter 1959–1960), 224–240; and Ernest van den Haag, "Social Science Testimony in the Desegregation Cases —A Reply to Professor Kenneth Clark," *Villanova Law Review,* 6 (Fall 1960), 69–79. Clark was chief of the social psychologists who conducted the demonstrations alleged to prove the deleterious effects of school segregation on black children.

The full oral arguments before the Supreme Court in the school cases, including the sharp questioning from the Bench, have been published under the title *Argument: The Oral Argument Before the Supreme Court in Brown* v. *Board of Education of Topeka* (New York, 1969), ed. by Leon Friedman.

The enforcement problems of *Brown* have been elaborately examined many times. A valuable symposium is John H. McCord, ed., *With All Deliberate Speed* (Urbana, Ill., 1969). Two different approaches from the standpoint of federal judges in the South are Jack W. Peltason, *Fifty-Eight Lonely Men: Southern Federal Judges and School Desegregation* (New York, 1962); and the report of a liberal southern judge, Frank M. Johnson, Jr., "School Desegregation Problems in the South: An Historical Perspective," *Minnesota Law Review,* 54 (June 1970), 1157–1173.

In respect to civil rights activism and black militance, the Court's expansion of traditional civil liberties (up to 1966) is extensively described in Milton R. Konvitz, *Expanding Liberties* (New York, 1967). See also Harry Kalven, Jr., *The Negro and the First Amendment* (Chicago, 1965). On the Court's partial retreat since 1966, the reader can find many interesting articles under the appropriate headings of the *Index to Legal Periodicals,* cumulated annually from monthly supplements. Another good source is the *Index to Periodical Articles Related to Law,* an annual publication.

The interested student new to the subject of the Supreme Court may wish to study some introductory histories on the role of the Court and some discussions of its functions. Very readable surveys that carry the story of the Court into the 1950s are Robert G. McCloskey's synthesis, *The American Supreme Court* (Chicago, 1961); Fred Rodell's sprightly *Nine Men: A Political History of the Supreme Court* (New York, 1955); and Alpheus T. Mason's *The Supreme Court: Palladium of Freedom* (Ann Arbor, Mich., 1962), which builds on the philosophy of the Bill of Rights. For the era of the Warren Court, see G. Theodore Mitau's well-organized *Decade of Decision: The Supreme Court and the Constitutional Revolution 1954–1964* (New York, 1967). The long-continuing debates over the proper role of judicial review are nicely summarized, with reprints of representative articles, in Leonard Levy, ed., *Judicial Review and the Supreme Court* (New York, 1967).